Bergsonism

Translated by Hugh Tomlinson

and Barbara Habberjam

Bergsonism

Gilles Deleuze

ZONE BOOKS · NEW YORK

1991

© 1988 Urzone, Inc.
ZONE BOOKS
633 Vanderbilt Street
Brooklyn, NY 11218

First Paperback Edition
Eighth Printing 2018

Originally published in France as *Le Bergsonisme*
© 1996 Presses Universitaires de France.

Printed in the United States of America.

Distributed by The MIT Press,
Cambridge, Massachusetts, and London, England

Library of Congress Cataloging-in-Publication Data

Deleuze, Gilles.
    [Bergsonisme. English].
    Bergsonism / Gilles Deleuze; translated by
    Hugh Tomlinson.
        p.   cm.
    Translation of: Bergsonisme.
    Bibliography: p.
ISBN 978-0-942299-07-8 (pbk.)
1. Bergson, Henry, 1859–1941. I. Title.
B2430.B4D3513 1988
194—DC19

                                        87-34051

Contents

Translator's Introduction   7

References to Bergson's Works   1 1

I   *Intuition as Method*   1 3

II   *Duration as Immediate Datum*   3 7

III   *Memory as Virtual Coexistence*   5 1

IV   *One or Many Durations?*   7 3

V   Élan Vital *as Movement of Differentiation*   9 1

A Return to Bergson   1 1 5

Notes   1 1 9

Index   1 3 7

This book was originally published in 1966 as part of a series of short studies known as "Initiation Philosophique." On first impression, the subject matter appears unpromising. Although Henri Bergson was one of the most important and widely read philosophers of the first decades of the twentieth century, nowadays his work seems to be almost forgotten. As Kolakowski says, "Today's philosophers, both in their research and in their teaching are almost entirely indifferent to his legacy."[1] Bergsonism is reduced to the status of a footnote in histories of philosophy, making a brief appearance in studies of "vitalism" or "irrationalism."

But this first impression is misleading. For Deleuze, Bergson forms part of a "counter history" of philosophy. He was a writer like Lucretius, Spinoza, Hume or Nietzsche "who seemed to be part of the history of philosophy, but who escaped from it in one respect or altogether."[2] In the 1950s and 1960s, it was writing about philosophers of this kind that enabled Deleuze to make his escape from the scholasticism of post-war French academic philosophy. He has described this task of escaping the history of philosophy as follows:

My way of getting out of it at that time, was, I really think, to conceive of the history of philosophy as a kind of buggery or, what comes to the same thing, immaculate conception. I imagined myself getting onto the back of an author, and giving him a child, which would be his and which would at the same time be a monster. It is very important that it should be his child, because the author actually had to say everything that I made him say. But it also had to be a monster because it was necessary to go through all kinds of decenterings, slips, break ins, secret emissions, which I really enjoyed. My book on Bergson seems to me a classic case of this.[3]

But Bergson is not just an exemplary target for the philosophical perversion of the early Deleuze. Bergson's work has provided Deleuze with materials for his own tool box, for the manufacture of his own concepts and his own war machines. As he said to Claire Parnet,

Bergson, of course, was also caught up in French-style history of philosophy, and yet in him there is something which cannot be assimilated, which enabled him to provide a shock, to be a rallying point for all the opposition, the object of so many hatreds: and this is not so much because of the theme of duration, as of the theory and practice of becomings of all kinds, of coexistent multiplicities.[4]

Deleuze has himself taken up and transformed these Bergsonian notions in his own errant campaigns for constructive pluralism, recently describing himself as an empiricist engaged in tracing the becomings of which multiplicities are made up.[5]

The affinities between Deleuze and Bergson led Gillian Rose to speak of his work as "the new Bergsonism."[6] But this may lead to a misunderstanding as Deleuze's work is characterized not by a fidelity to any master, but by a series of transformations of concepts borrowed from a range of writers from many disciplines. Nevertheless, Deleuze and Bergson do have a number of important "problems" in common. In particular, Deleuze's work has been increasingly preoccupied with the problems of "movement" and "time" which so concerned Bergson. His recent isolation of the cinematographic concepts of the "movement-image" and the "time-image" grows out of four "commentaries" on Bergson's notions of movement, image, recognition and time.[7]

The translation of the Bergsonian terms in the book presents a special difficulty. Bergson's mother was from the north of England and he spoke the language from childhood. Many of his major works were translated during his lifetime and personally revised by him.[8] We have not followed the terminology adopted in these translations in three respects.

First, in the authorized translations, the key term "*élan vital*" is rendered as "vital impetus." This version is not an entirely happy one and has often been criticized. The French word "*élan*" has a much broader range of sense than the English "impetus," from "momentum" through "surge" to "vigor." We have thus followed the practice of recent writers on Bergson and have left "*élan vital*" in the French. Second, the authorized translations do not make a systematic distinction between "recollection" and "memory" in the English. We have invariably rendered "*souvenir*" as "recollection" and "*mémoire*" as "memory" and have altered extracts from the Bergson translations accordingly. Third, the authorized translations have used an English neologism "detension," as their rendering of the word "*détente*." However, this only suggests one of the range of senses in which Bergson uses the word, that is "relaxation," in contrast to "contraction" (in other words, "de-tension") – the Nixon–Brezhnev sense. It does not, however, convey the more active senses of the word: meaning "spring" or "expansion." Bergson often draws on this last sense which is used technically in thermodynamics to mean the expansion of a gas that has been previously subject to pressure. We have therefore rendered "*détente*" by either "relaxation" or "expansion" depending on the context, with the original in parentheses.

We have followed the authorized translations in translating "*durée*" as "duration" and adopting "extensity" and "extension" to translate Bergson's terms "*étendue*" and "*extension*." We have translated both "*écart*" and "*intervalle*" as "interval" with the French word in parentheses. Deleuze often uses Kant's distinction between the "*quaestio quid juris*" and the "*quaestio quid facti*," between the "*question de droit*" and the "*question de fait*."[9] We have translated "*en fait*" and "*en droit*" by "in fact" and "in principle."

We are grateful to Urzone, Inc. and particularly to Ramona Naddaff for suggesting that we translate this book. A number of friends and colleagues have made suggestions and comments and tried to remind us how English is supposed to read. In particular we would like to thank: Caroline Davidson, Robert Galeta, Martin Joughin and Richard Williams.

Hugh Tomlinson
Barbara Habberjam
London,
December 1987

References to Bergson's Works

TF *Time and Free Will*, translated by F.L. Pogson, London: George Allen & Unwin Ltd. New York: Macmillan & Co., 1919. *Essai sur les données immédiates de la conscience*, 1889.

MM *Matter and Memory*, translated by Nancy Margaret Paul and W. Scott Palmer, London: George Allen & Unwin Ltd., 1911. *Matière et Mémoire*, 1896.

CE *Creative Evolution*, translated by Arthur Mitchell, New York: Henry Holt & Co., 1911 (New York: Macmillan & Co., 1944). *L'Evolution créatrice*, 1907.

ME *Mind-Energy*, translated by H. Wildon Carr, New York: Henry Holt & Co., 1920. *L'Energie spirituelle*, 1919.

DS *Duration and Simultaneity*, translated by Leon Jacobson, Indianapolis: Bobbs-Merrill, 1965. *Durée et Simultanéité*, 1922.

MR *The Two Sources of Morality and Religion*, translated by R. Ashley Audra and Cloudesley Brereton with the assistance of W. Horsfall Carter, New York: Henry Holt & Co., 1935. *Les deux sources de la morale et de la religion*, 1932.

CM *The Creative Mind*, translated by Mabelle L. Andison, Westport, Connecticut: Greenwood Press, 1946. *La Pensée et le Mouvant*, 1941.

References to the original French are in parentheses. The DS references are to the 4th Edition. For all the other works, the French references are, first, to the Centenary Edition (Presses Universitaires de France), and then to the 1939–1941 reprints.

CHAPTER I

Intuition as Method

Duration, Memory, *Élan Vital* mark the major stages of Bergson's philosophy. This book sets out to determine, first, the relationship between these three notions and, second, the progress they involve.

Intuition is the method of Bergsonism. Intuition is neither a feeling, an inspiration, nor a disorderly sympathy, but a fully developed method, one of the most fully developed methods in philosophy. It has its strict rules, constituting that which Bergson calls "precision" in philosophy. Bergson emphasizes this point: Intuition, as he understands it methodologically, already presupposes *duration*. "These conclusions on the subject of duration were, as it seemed to me, decisive. Step by step they led me to raise intuition to the level of a philosophical method. The use of the word intuition, however, caused me some degree of hesitation."[1] And to Höffding, he writes: "The theory of intuition which you stress more than that of duration only became clear to me long afterwards."[2]

But first and second have many meanings. Intuition certainly is second in relation to duration or to memory. But while these notions by themselves denote lived realities and experiences, they do not give us any means of *knowing* (*connaître*) them with a precision analogous to that of science. We might say, strangely enough, that duration would remain purely intuitive, in the ordinary sense of the word, if intuition — in the properly Bergsonian sense — were not there as method. The fact is that Bergson relied on the intuitive method to establish philosophy as an absolutely "precise" discipline, as precise in *its* field, as capable of being prolonged and transmitted as science itself is. And without the methodical thread of intuition, the relationships between Duration, Memory and *Élan Vital* would themselves remain indeterminate from the point of view of knowledge. In all of these respects, we must bring intuition as rigorous or precise method to the forefront of our discussion.[3]

The most general methodological question is this: How is intuition — which primarily denotes an immediate knowledge (*connaissance*) — capable of forming a method, once it is accepted that the method essentially involves one or several mediations? Bergson often presents intuition as a simple act. But, in his view, simplicity does not exclude a qualitative and virtual multiplicity, various directions in which it comes to be actualized. It is in this sense, then, that intuition involves a plurality of meanings and irreducible multiple aspects.[4] Bergson distinguishes essentially three distinct sorts of acts that in turn determine the rules of the method: The first concerns the stating and creating of problems; the second, the discovery of genuine differences in kind; the third, the apprehension of real time. It is by showing how we move from one meaning to another and what the "fundamental meaning" is, that we are able to rediscover the simplicity of intuition as lived act, and thus answer the general methodological question.

*   *   *

FIRST RULE: *Apply the test of true and false to problems themselves. Condemn false problems and reconcile truth and creation at the level of problems.*

We are wrong to believe that the true and the false can only be brought to bear on solutions, that they only begin with solutions. This prejudice is social (for society, and the language that transmits its order-words [*mots d'ordre*], "set up" [*donnent*] ready-made problems, as if they were drawn out of "the city's administrative filing cabinets," and force us to "solve" them, leaving us only a thin margin of freedom). Moreover, this prejudice goes back to childhood, to the classroom: It is the school teacher who "poses" the problems; the pupil's task is to discover the solutions. In this way we are kept in a kind of slavery. True freedom lies in a power to decide, to constitute problems themselves. And this "semi-divine" power entails the disappearance of false problems as much as the creative upsurge of true ones. "The truth is that in philosophy and even elsewhere it is a question of *finding* the problem and consequently of *positing* it, even more than of solving it. For a speculative problem is solved as soon as it is properly stated. By that I mean that its solution exists then, although it may remain hidden and, so to speak, covered up: The only thing left to do is to *uncover* it. But stating the problem is not simply uncovering, it is inventing. Discovery, or uncovering, has to do with what already exists, actually or virtually; it was therefore certain to happen sooner or later. Invention gives being to what did not exist; it might never have happened. Already in mathematics, and still more in metaphysics, the effort of invention consists most often in raising the problem, in creating the terms in which it will be stated. The stating and solving of the prob-

15

lem are here very close to being equivalent: The truly great problems are set forth only when they are solved."[5]

It is not just the whole history of mathematics that supports Bergson. We might compare the last sentence of this extract from Bergson with Marx's formulation, which is valid for practice itself: "Humanity only sets itself problems that it is capable of solving." In neither example is it a case of saying that problems are like the shadow of pre-existing solutions (the whole context suggests the contrary). Nor is it a case of saying that only the problems count. On the contrary, it is the solution that counts, but the problem always has the solution it deserves, in terms of the way in which it is stated (i.e., the conditions under which it is determined as problem), and of the means and terms at our disposal for stating it. In this sense, the history of man, from the theoretical as much as from the practical point of view is that of the construction of problems. It is here that humanity makes its own history, and the becoming conscious of that activity is like the conquest of freedom. (It is true that, in Bergson, the very notion of the problem has its roots beyond history, in life itself or in the *élan vital*: Life is essentially determined in the act of avoiding obstacles, stating and solving a problem. The construction of the organism is both the stating of a problem and a solution.)[6]

But how can this constitutive power which resides in the problem be reconciled with a norm of the true? While it is relatively easy to define the true and the false in relation to solutions whose problems have already been stated, it seems much more difficult to say in what the true and the false consist when applied to the process of stating problems. This is how many philosophers fall into circular arguments: Conscious of the need to take the test of true and false beyond solutions

16

into problems themselves, they are content to define the truth or falsity of a problem by the possibility or impossibility of its being solved. Bergson's great virtue, on the other hand, is to have attempted an intrinsic determination of the false in the expression "false problem." This is the source of a rule that is complementary to the preceding general rule.

COMPLEMENTARY RULE: *False problems are of two sorts, "nonexistent problems," defined as problems whose very terms contain a confusion of the "more" and the "less"; and "badly stated" questions, so defined because their terms represent badly analyzed composites.*

To illustrate the first kind of problem Bergson cites the problems of nonbeing, of disorder or of the possible (the problems of knowledge and being); as examples of the second type, there are the problems of freedom or of intensity.[7] His analyses of these are famous. In the first case, they consist in showing that there is not *less*, but *more* in the idea of nonbeing than that of being, in disorder than in order, in the possible than in the real. In the idea of nonbeing there is in fact the idea of being, plus a logical operation of generalized negation, plus the particular psychological motive for that operation (such as when a being does not correspond to our expectation and we grasp it purely as the lack, the absence of what interests us). In the idea of disorder there is already the idea of order, plus its negation, plus the motive for that negation (when we encounter an order that is not the one we expected). And there is more in the idea of the possible than there is in the idea of the real: "For the possible is only the real with the addition of an act of mind that throws its image back into the past once it has been enacted," and the motive of that act (when we confuse

17

the upsurge of a reality in the universe with a succession of states in a closed system).[8]

When we ask "Why is there something rather than nothing?" or "Why is there order rather than disorder?" or "Why is there this rather than that (when that was equally possible)?" we fall into the same error: We mistake the more for the less, we behave as though nonbeing existed before being, disorder before order and the possible before existence. As though being came to fill in a void, order to organize a preceding disorder, the real to realize a primary possibility. Being, order or the existent are truth itself; but in the false problem there is a fundamental illusion, a "retrograde movement of the true," according to which being, order and the existent are supposed to precede themselves, or to precede the creative act that constitutes them, by projecting an image of themselves back into a possibility, a disorder, a nonbeing which are supposed to be primordial. This theme is a central one in Bergson's philosophy: It sums up his critique of the negative and of negation, in all its forms as sources of false problems.

Badly stated problems, the second type of false problem, introduce a different mechanism: This time it is a case of badly analyzed composites that arbitrarily group things that *differ in kind*. Take for example, the question of whether happiness is reducible to pleasure or not: Perhaps the term pleasure subsumes very varied irreducible states, just like the idea of happiness. If the terms do not correspond to "natural articulations" then the problem is false, for it does not affect "the very nature of things."[9] Here again, Bergson's analyses are famous: for example, the one in which he condemns intensity as such a composite. Whether the quality of the sensation is confused with the muscular space that corresponds to it, or with the quantity of the physical cause that produces it, the notion of intensity involves an impure mixture between determinations that differ in kind, so that the question "by how much does the sensation grow?" always goes back to a badly stated problem.[10] Likewise the problem of freedom, in which two types of "multiplicity" are confused: that of terms juxtaposed in space and that of states which merge together in duration.

Let us return to the first type of false problem. Here, Bergson says, the more is mistaken for the less. But there are also times when Bergson says that the less here is mistaken for the more: just as doubt about an action only apparently adds to the action, when in reality it indicates a half-willing; negation is not added to *what it denies*, but only indicates a weakness in *the person who denies*. "For we feel that a divinely created will or thought is too full of itself, in the immensity of its reality, to have the slightest idea of a lack of order or a lack of being. To imagine the possibility of absolute disorder, all the more the possibility of nothingness, would be for it to say to itself that it might not have existed at all, and that would be a weakness incompatible with its nature, which is force.... It is not something more but something less; it is a deficit of the will."[11] Is there a contradiction between these two formulations, where nonbeing is sometimes presented as a more in relation to being and sometimes as a less? There is no contradiction if we bear in mind that what Bergson is condemning in nonexistent problems is the obsession *in all its aspects* with thinking in terms of more and less. The idea of disorder appears when, instead of seeing that there are two or more irreducible orders (for example, that of life and that of mechanism, each present when the other is absent), we retain only a general idea of order that we confine ourselves to opposing to disorder and to thinking in correlation with the idea of disorder. The idea of nonbeing appears when, instead of grasping the different realities that are indefinitely substituted for one another, we muddle them together in the homogeneity of a Being in general, which can only be opposed to nothingness, be related to nothingness. The idea of the possible appears when, instead of grasping each existent in its novelty, the whole of existence is related to a pre-formed element, from which everything is supposed to emerge by simple "realization."

In short, each time that we think in terms of more or less, we have already disregarded the differences in kind between the two orders, or between beings, between existents. In this way *we can see how the first type of false problem rests, in the final analysis, on the second*: The idea of disorder emerges from a general idea of order as badly analyzed composite, etc. And conceiving everything in terms of more and less, seeing nothing but differences in degree or differences in intensity where, more profoundly, there are differences in kind is perhaps the most general error of thought, the error common to science and metaphysics.

We are therefore victims of a fundamental illusion that corresponds to the two aspects of the false problem. The very notion of the false problem indeed implies that we have to struggle not against simple mistakes (false solutions), but against something more profound: an illusion that carries us along, or in which we are immersed, inseparable from our condition. A mirage, as Bergson describes the projection backward of the possible. Bergson borrows an idea from Kant although he completely transforms it: It was Kant who showed that reason deep within itself engenders not mistakes but *inevitable* illusions, only the effect of which could be warded off. Although Bergson determines the nature of false problems in a completely different way and although the Kantian critique itself seems to him to be a collection of badly stated problems, he treats the illusion in a way similar to Kant. The illusion is based in the deepest part of the intelligence: It is not, strictly speaking, dispelled or dispellable, rather it can only be *repressed*.[12] We tend to think in terms of more and less, that is, to see differences in degree where there are differences in kind. We can only react against this intellectual tendency by bringing to life, again *in* the intelligence, another tendency, which is critical. But where, precisely, does this second tendency come from? Only intuition can produce and activate it, because it rediscovers differences in kind beneath the differences in degree, and conveys to the intelligence the criteria that enable it to distinguish between true and false problems. Bergson shows clearly that the intelligence is the faculty that states problems in general (the instinct is rather a faculty for finding solutions).[13] But only intuition decides between the true and the false in the problems that are stated, even if this means driving the intelligence to turn back against itself.

★   ★   ★

SECOND RULE: *Struggle against illusion, rediscover the true differences in kind or articulations of the real.*[14]

The Bergsonian dualisms are famous: duration–space, quality–quantity, heterogeneous–homogeneous, continuous–discontinuous, the two multiplicities, memory–matter, recollection–perception, contraction–relaxation* (*détente*), instinct–intelligence, the two sources, etc. Even the running heads that

---

*For a discussion of the problem of translating *détente*, see Preface (Trans.).

Bergson puts at the top of each page of his books indicate his taste for dualisms – which do not, however, have the last word in his philosophy. What, therefore, do they mean? According to Bergson, a composite must always be divided according to its natural articulations, that is, into elements which differ in kind. Intuition as method is a method of division, Platonic in inspiration. Bergson is aware that things are mixed together in reality; in fact, experience itself offers us nothing but composites. But that is not where the difficulty lies. For example, we make time into a representation imbued with space. The awkward thing is that we no longer know how to distinguish in that *representation* the two component elements which differ in kind, the two pure *presences* of duration and extensity. We mix extensity and duration so thoroughly that we can now only oppose their mixture to a principle that is assumed to be both nonspatial and nontemporal, and in relation to which space and time, duration and extensity, are now only deteriorations.[15] To take yet another example, we mix recollection and perception; but we do not know how to recognize what goes back to perception and what goes back to recollection. We no longer distinguish the two pure presences of matter and memory in representation, and we no longer see anything but differences in degree between perception–recollections and recollection-perceptions. In short, we measure the mixtures with a unit that is itself impure and already mixed. We have lost the ground of composites. The obsession with the *pure* in Bergson goes back to this restoration of differences in kind. Only that which differs in kind can be said to be pure, but only *tendencies* differ in kind.[16] The composite must therefore be divided according to qualitative and qualified tendencies, that is, according to the way in which it combines duration and extensity as they are

22

defined as movements, directions of movements (hence dura-tion–contraction and matter–expansion [*détente*]). Again, there is some resemblance between intuition as method of division and transcendental analysis: If the composite represents the fact, it must be divided into tendencies or into pure presences that only exist *in principle* (*en droit*).[17] We go beyond experience, toward the conditions of experience (but these are not, in the Kantian manner, the conditions of all possible experience: They are the conditions of real experience).

This is the Bergsonian leitmotif: People have seen only dif-ferences in degree where there are differences in kind. And Bergson groups his major critiques, which take many differ-ent forms, under this heading. His fundamental criticism of metaphysics is that it sees differences in degree between a spatialized time and an eternity which it assumes to be primary (time as deterioration, relaxation [*détente*] or diminution of being...): All beings are defined on a scale of intensity, between the two extremes of perfection and nothingness. But he directs a similar criticism at science; there is no definition of *mechanism* other than that which invokes a spatialized time, according to which beings no longer present anything but differences of degree, of position, of dimension, of proportion. There is even "mechanism" in evolutionism, to the extent that it postulates a unilinear evolution and takes us from one living organization to another by simple intermediaries, transitions and variations of degree. The whole source of the false problems and the illusions that overwhelm us lies in this disregard for true dif-ferences in kind: As early as the first chapter of *Matter and Memory*, Bergson shows how the forgetting of differences in kind — on the one hand between perception and affection, on the other hand between perception and recollection — gives

23

rise to all kinds of false problems by making us think that our perception is inextensive in character: "There are, in the idea that we project outside ourselves states which are purely internal, so many misconceptions, so many lame answers to badly stated questions...."[18]

No text shows more clearly than this first chapter of *Matter and Memory* how complex the manipulation of intuition is as a method of division. The representation has to be divided into the elements that condition it, into pure presences or tendencies that differ in kind. How does Bergson proceed? He asks, first, between what two things there may be (or may not be) a difference in kind. His first response is that, since the brain is an "image" among other images, or ensures certain movements among other movements, *there cannot be* a difference in kind between the faculty of the brain which is said to be perceptive and the reflex functions of the core. Thus, the brain does not manufacture representations, but only complicates the relationship between a received movement (excitation) and an executed movement (response). Between the two, it establishes an interval (*écart*), whether it divides up the received movement infinitely or prolongs it in a plurality of possible reactions. Even if recollections take advantage of this interval or, strictly speaking, "interpolate themselves," nothing changes. We can, for the moment, discount them as being involved in another "line." On the line that we are tracing, we only have, we can only have matter and movement, movement which is more or less complicated, more or less delayed. The whole question is knowing whether, in this way, we also already have perception. By virtue of the cerebral interval, in effect, a being can retain from a material object and the actions issuing from it only those elements that interest him.[19] So that perception

24

is not the object *plus* something, but the object *minus* something, minus everything that does not interest us. It could be said that the object itself merges with a *pure* virtual perception, at the same time as our real perception merges with the object from which it has abstracted only that which did not interest us. Hence Bergson's famous thesis (the full consequences of which we will have to analyze): We perceive things where they are, perception puts us at once into matter, is impersonal, and coincides with the perceived object. Continuing on this same line, the whole of Bergson's method consists, first of all, in seeking the terms between which *there could not* be a difference in kind: There cannot be a difference in kind, but only a difference in degree between the faculty of the brain and the function of the core, between the perception of matter and matter itself.

We are now in a position to trace out the second line, which differs in kind from the first. In order to establish the first we needed *fictions*: We assumed that the body was like a pure mathematical point in space, a pure instant, or a succession of instants in time. But these fictions were not simply hypotheses: They consisted in pushing beyond experience a direction drawn from experience itself. It is only in this way that we can extract a whole aspect of the conditions of experience. All that is left now is to ask ourselves what fills up the cerebral interval, what takes advantage of it to become embodied. Bergson's response is three-fold. First, there is affectivity, which assumes that the body *is* something other than a mathematical point and which gives it volume in space. Next, it is the recollections of memory that link the instants to each other and interpolate the past in the present. Finally, it is memory again in another form, in the form of a contraction of matter that makes the quality appear. (It is therefore memory that makes the body something other than instantaneous and gives it a duration in time). We are consequently in the presence of a new line, that of subjectivity, on which affectivity, recollection-memory, and contraction-memory are ranged: These terms may be said to differ in kind from those of the preceding line (perception-object-matter).[20] In short, representation in general is divided into two directions that differ in kind, into two pure presences that do not allow themselves to be represented: that of perception which puts us *at once* into matter and that of memory which puts us *at once* into the mind. Once again, the question is not whether the two lines meet and mix together. This mixture is our experience itself, our representation. But all our false problems derive from the fact that we do not know how to go beyond experience toward the conditions of experience, toward the articulations of the real, and rediscover what differs in kind in the composites that are given to us and on which we live. These two acts, perception and recollection, "always interpenetrate each other, are always exchanging something of their substance as by a process of endosmosis. The proper office of psychologists would be to dissociate them, to give back to each its natural purity; in this way many difficulties raised by psychology and perhaps also by metaphysics might be lessened. But they will have it that these mixed states, compounded, in unequal proportions, of pure perception and pure recollection, are simple. And so we are condemned to an ignorance alike of pure recollection and of pure perception, to knowing only a single kind of phenomenon that will be called now recollection and now perception, according to the predominance in it of one or other of the two aspects; and, consequently, to finding between

26

perception and recollection only a difference in degree and not in kind."[21]

Intuition leads us to go beyond the state of experience toward the conditions of experience. But these conditions are neither general nor abstract. They are no broader than the conditioned: they are the conditions of real experience. Bergson speaks of going "to seek experience at its source, or rather above that decisive *turn*, where, taking a bias in the direction of our utility, it becomes properly *human* experience."[22] Above the turn is precisely the point at which we finally discover differences in kind. But there are so many difficulties in trying to reach this focal point that the acts of intuition, which are apparently contradictory, have to be multiplied. Bergson, thus, sometimes speaks of a movement that is exactly appropriate to the experience, sometimes a broadening out, sometimes a tightening and narrowing. For, in the first place, the determination of each "line" involves a sort of contradiction in which apparently diverse facts are grouped according to their natural affinities, drawn together according to their articulation. But, on the other hand, we push each line beyond the turn, to the point where it goes beyond our own experience: an extraordinary broadening out that forces us to think a pure perception identical to the whole of matter, a pure memory identical to the totality of the past. It is in this sense that Bergson on several occasions compares the approach of philosophy to the procedure of infinitesimal calculus: When we have benefitted in experience from a little light which shows us a line of articulation, all that remains is to extend it beyond experience – just as mathematicians reconstitute, with the infinitely small elements that they perceive of the real curve, "the curve itself stretching out into the darkness behind them."[23] In any case,

Bergson is not one of those philosophers who ascribes a properly human wisdom and equilibrium to philosophy. To open
us up to the inhuman and the superhuman (*durations* which are
inferior or superior to our own), to go beyond the human condition: This is the meaning of philosophy, in so far as our condition condemns us to live among badly analyzed composites,
and to be badly analyzed composites ourselves.[24]

But this broadening out, or even this going-beyond does not
consist in going beyond experience toward concepts. For concepts only define, in the Kantian manner, the conditions of all
possible experience in general. Here, on the other hand, it is
a case of real experience in all its peculiarities. And if we must
broaden it, or even go beyond it, this is only in order to find
the articulations on which these peculiarities depend. So that
the conditions of experience are less determined in concepts
than in pure percepts.[25] And, while these percepts themselves
are united in a concept, it is a concept modeled on the thing
itself, which only suits that thing, and which, in this sense, is
no broader than what it must account for. For when we have
followed each of the "lines" beyond the turn in experience,
we must also rediscover the point at which they intersect again,
where the directions cross and where the tendencies that differ in kind link together again to give rise to the thing as we
know it. It might be thought that nothing is easier, and that
experience itself has already given us this point. But it is not
as simple as that. After we have followed the lines of divergence
beyond the turn, these lines must intersect again, not at the point
from which we started, but rather at a virtual point, at a virtual
image of the point of departure, which is itself located beyond
the turn in experience; and which finally gives us the sufficient
reason of the thing, the sufficient reason of the composite, the

sufficient reason of the point of departure. So that the expression "beyond the decisive turn" has two meanings: First, it denotes the moment when the lines, setting out from an uncertain common point given in experience, diverge increasingly according to the differences in kind. Then, it denotes another moment when these lines converge again to give us this time the virtual image or the distinct reason of the common point. Turn and return. Dualism is therefore only a moment, which must lead to the re-formation of a monism. This is why, after the broadening out, a final narrowing follows, just as integration follows differentiation. "We have alluded elsewhere to those 'lines of fact,' each one indicating but the direction of truth, because it does not go far enough: Truth itself, however, will be reached if two of them can be prolonged to the point where they intersect.... In our opinion this method of intersection is the only one that can bring about a decisive advance in metaphysics."[26] There are, therefore, two successive turns in experience as it were, both in a reverse direction: They constitute what Bergson calls *precision* in philosophy.

Hence, a COMPLEMENTARY RULE *to the second rule: The real is not only that which is cut out (*se découpe*) according to natural articulations or differences in kind; it is also that which intersects again (*se récoupe*) along paths converging toward the same ideal or virtual point.*

The particular function of this rule is to show how a problem, when it is properly stated, tends to be solved of its own accord. For example, still in the first chapter of *Matter and Memory*, the problem of memory is correctly stated, since, starting from the perception–recollection composite, we divide this composite into two divergent and expanded directions which correspond to a true difference in kind between soul and body, spirit and matter. But we can only reach the solution to the problem by narrowing: When we attain the original point at which the two divergent directions converge again, the precise point at which recollection inserts itself into perception, the virtual point that is like the reflection and the reason of the departure point. Thus the problem of soul and body, of matter and spirit, is only solved by an extreme narrowing in which Bergson shows how the lines of objectivity and of subjectivity, the lines of external observation and of internal experience, must converge at the end of their different processes, all the way to the case of aphasia.[27]

Bergson shows, similarly, that the problem of the immortality of the soul tends to be solved by the convergence of two very different lines: that of an experience of memory and that of a quite different, mystical, experience.[28] The problems that are unraveled at the point at which *three* lines of facts converge are even more complex: Such is the nature of consciousness in the first chapter of *Mind-Energy*. It should be noted that this method of intersection forms a genuine probabilism: Each line defines a probability.[29] But it is a qualitative probabilism, lines of fact being qualitatively distinct. In their divergence, in the disarticulation of the real that they brought about according to the differences in kind, they already constituted a superior empiricism, capable of stating problems and of going beyond experience toward concrete conditions. In their convergence, in the intersection of the real to which they proceed, they now define a superior probabilism, one capable of solving problems and of bringing the condition back to the conditioned so that no distance remains between them.

*　　*　　*

30

THIRD RULE: *State problems and solve them in terms of time rather than of space.*[30]

This rule gives the "fundamental meaning" of intuition: Intuition presupposes duration, it consists in thinking in terms of duration.[31] We can only understand it by returning to the movement of the division determining the differences in kind. At first sight it would seem that a difference in kind is established between two things, or rather between two tendencies. This is true, but only superficially. Let us consider the principal Bergsonian division: that between duration and space. All the other divisions, all the other dualisms involve it, derive from it, or result in it. Now, we cannot simply confine ourselves to affirming a difference in kind between duration and space. The division occurs between (1) duration, which "tends" for its part to take on or bear all the differences in kind (because it is endowed with the power of qualitatively varying with itself), and (2) space, which never presents anything but differences of degree (since it is quantitative homogeneity). There is thus not a difference in kind between the two halves of the division; the qualitative difference is entirely on one side. When we divide something up according to its natural articulations (as with proportions and figures that vary greatly from case to case), we have: on the one hand, the aspect of space, by which the thing can only ever differ in degree from other things *and from itself* (augmentation, diminution); and on the other hand, the aspect of duration, by which the thing differs in kind from all others *and from itself* (alteration).

Take a lump of sugar: It has a spatial configuration. But if we approach it from that angle, all we will ever grasp are differences in degree between that sugar and any other thing. But

31

it also has a duration, a rhythm of duration, a way of being in time that is at least partially revealed in the process of its dissolving, and that shows how this sugar differs in kind not only from other things, but first and foremost from itself. This alteration, which is one with the essence or the substance of a thing, is what we grasp when we conceive of it in terms of Duration. In this respect, Bergson's famous formulation, "I must wait until the sugar dissolves" has a still broader meaning than is given to it by its context.[32] It signifies that my own duration, such as I live it in the impatience of waiting, for example, serves to reveal other durations that beat to other rhythms, that differ in kind from mine. Duration is always the location and the environment of differences in kind; it is even their totality and multiplicity. There are no differences in kind except in duration — while space is nothing other than the location, the environment, the totality of differences in degree.

Perhaps we now have the means to resolve the most general of methodological questions. When Plato formulated his method of division, he too intended to divide a composite into two halves, or along several lines. But the whole problem lay in knowing how to choose the right half: Why was what we were looking for on one side rather than on the other? Division could therefore be criticized for not being a genuine method since it lacked a "middle term" and still depended on an inspiration. In Bergsonism, the difficulty seems to disappear. For by dividing the composite according to two tendencies, with only one showing the way in which a thing varies qualitatively in time, Bergson effectively gives himself the means of choosing the "right side" in each case; that of the essence. In short, intuition has become method, or rather method has been reconciled with the immediate. Intuition is not duration

32

itself. Intuition is rather the movement by which we emerge
from our own duration, by which we make use of our own duration to affirm and immediately to recognize the existence of
other durations, above or below us. "Only the method of which
we are speaking allows one to pass beyond idealism as well as
realism, to affirm the existence of objects both inferior and
superior to us, though nevertheless, in a certain sense, interior to us.... One perceives any number of durations, all very
different from one another" (in fact the words *inferior* and *superior*
should not mislead us, they denote differences in kind).[33] Without intuition as method, duration would remain a simple psychological experience. Conversely, if it did not coincide with
duration, intuition would not be capable of carrying out the
program that corresponds to the preceding rules: the determination of true problems or of genuine differences in kind....

Let us return, therefore, to the illusion of false problems.
Where does it come from and in what sense is it inevitable?
Bergson calls into question the order of needs, of action, and
of society that predisposes us to retain only what interests us
in things; the order of intelligence, in its natural affinity with
space; and the order of general ideas that tends to obscure differences in kind. Or rather there are very varied general ideas
that themselves differ in kind, some referring to objective
resemblances in living bodies, others to objective identities
in inanimate bodies, and others again to subjective demands
in manufactured objects. But we are quick to form a general
idea of all general ideas and to dissolve differences in kind in
this element of generality.[34] "We make differences in kind melt
into the homogeneity of the space which subtends them."[35]
It is true that this collection of reasons is still psychological
and inseparable from our own condition. We must take into

consideration more profound reasons. For while the idea of a homogeneous space implies a sort of artifice or symbol separating us from reality, it is nevertheless the case that matter and extensity are realities, themselves prefiguring the order of space. Although it is illusion, space is not merely grounded in our nature, but in the nature of things. Matter is effectively the "aspect" by which things tend to present to each other, and to us, only differences in degree. Experience gives us composites. Now the state of the composite does not consist only in uniting elements that differ in kind, but in uniting them in conditions such that these constituent differences in kind *cannot be* grasped in it. In short, there is a point of view, or rather a state of things, in which differences in kind can no longer appear. The *retrograde movement* of the true is not merely an illusion *about* the true, but belongs *to* the true itself. Bergson adds (dividing the composite "religion" into two directions – static and dynamic religion) that in placing ourselves at a certain standpoint "we should perceive a series of transitions and, as it were, differences of degree, whereas really there is a radical difference in kind."[36]

The illusion, therefore, does not result only from our nature, but from the world in which we live, from the side of being that manifests itself to us in the first place. Bergson evolved, in a certain sense, from the beginning to the end of his work. The two major aspects of his evolution are the following: Duration seemed to him to be less and less reducible to a psychological experience and became instead the variable essence of things, providing the theme of a complex ontology. But, simultaneously, space seemed to him to be less and less reducible to a fiction separating us from this psychological reality, rather, it was itself grounded in being and expressed one of its two slopes, one of its two directions. The absolute, said Bergson, has two *sides* (aspects): spirit imbued with metaphysics and matter known by science.[37] But the point is that science is not a relative knowledge, a symbolic discipline that commends itself only by its successes or its effectiveness; science is part of ontology, it is one of ontology's two halves. The Absolute is difference, but difference has two facets, differences in degree and differences in kind. It can, therefore, be seen that when we grasp simple differences in degree between things, when science itself invites us to see the world in this way, we are again in an absolute ("With modern physics more and more clearly revealing to us differences in number behind our distinctions of quality....").[38] It is, however, an illusion. But it is only an illusion to the extent that we project the real landscape of the first slope onto the other. If the illusion can be repressed it is because of that other slope, that of duration, which gives us differences in kind *corresponding in the final instance* to differences of proportion as they appear in space, and already in matter and extension.

*   *   *

Thus intuition does form a method with its three (or five) rules. This is an essentially *problematizing* method (a critique of false problems and the invention of genuine ones), *differentiating* (carvings out and intersections), *temporalizing* (thinking in terms of duration). But how does intuition presuppose duration, and how, on the other hand, does it give duration a new extension from the point of view of being and knowledge? This is what remains to be determined.

CHAPTER II

Duration as Immediate Datum

We shall assume that the reader is familiar with the description of duration as psychological experience as it appears in *Time and Free Will* and in the first pages of *Creative Evolution*: It is a case of a "transition," of a "change," a *becoming*, but it is a becoming that endures, a change that is substance itself. The reader will note that Bergson has no difficulty in reconciling the two fundamental characteristics of duration; continuity and heterogeneity.[1] However, defined in this way, duration is not merely lived experience; it is also experience enlarged or even gone beyond; it is already a condition of experience. For experience always gives us a composite of space and duration. Pure duration offers us a succession that is purely internal, without exteriority; space, an exteriority without succession (in effect, this is the memory of the past; the recollection of what has happened in space would already imply a mind that endures). The two combine, and into this combination space introduces the forms of its extrinsic distinctions or of its homogeneous *and* discontinuous "sections," while duration contributes an internal succession that is both heterogeneous *and* continuous. We are thus able to "preserve" the instantaneous states of space and to juxtapose them in a sort of "auxiliary space": But we also introduce extrinsic distinctions into our duration; we decompose it into external parts and align it in a sort of homogeneous time. A composite of this kind (where homogeneous time merges with auxiliary space) must be divided up. Even before Bergson had become conscious of intuition as method, he had to face the task of dividing up the composite. Should it be divided along two pure directions? So long as Bergson does not explicitly pose the problem of an ontological origin of space, it is rather a case of dividing the composite in two directions, only one of which (duration) is pure, the other (space) is the impurity that denatures it.[2] Duration will be attained as "immediate datum" because it is associated with the right side, the good side of the composite.

The important thing here is that the decomposition of the composite reveals to us two types of multiplicity. One is represented by space (or rather, if all the nuances are taken into account, by the impure combination of homogeneous time): It is a multiplicity of exteriority, of simultaneity, of juxtaposition, of order, of quantitative differentiation, of *difference in degree*; it is a numerical multiplicity, *discontinuous and actual*. The other type of multiplicity appears in pure duration: It is an internal multiplicity of succession, of fusion, of organization, of heterogeneity, of qualitative discrimination, or of *difference in kind*; it is a *virtual and continuous* multiplicity that cannot be reduced to numbers.[3]

* * *

Too little importance has been attached to the use of this word "multiplicity." It is not part of the traditional vocabulary at all – this is particularly not the case when denoting a *continuum*. We

shall see not only that it is fundamental in terms of the construction of the method, but also that, even at this early stage,
it tells us about the problems that appear in *Time and Free Will*.
(These will be developed later). The word "multiplicity" is
not there as a vague noun corresponding to the well-known
philosophical notion of the Multiple in general. In fact *for
Bergson it is not a question of opposing the Multiple to the One but,
on the contrary, of distinguishing two types of multiplicity*. Now, this
problem goes back to a scholar of genius, G.B.R. Riemann, a
physicist and mathematician. Riemann defined as "multiplicities" those things that could be determined in terms of their
dimensions or their independent variables. He distinguished
discrete multiplicities and *continuous multiplicities*. The former contain the principle of their own metrics (the measure of one of
their parts being given by the number of elements they contain). The latter found a metrical principle in something else,
even if only in phenomena unfolding in them or in the forces
acting in them.[4] It is clear that Bergson, as a philosopher, was
well aware of Riemann's general problems. Not only his interest in mathematics points toward this, but, more specifically,
Duration and Simultaneity is a book in which Bergson opposes
his own doctrine to the theory of Relativity, which is directly
dependent on Riemann. If our hypothesis is correct, this book
loses its doubly strange character. In the first place, it does not
appear abruptly and without explanation. Rather, it brings into
the open a confrontation that until then, had been implicit
between Riemannian and Bergsonian interpretations of continuous multiplicities. Second, Bergson's renunciation and con-
demnation of this book is perhaps due to the fact that he did
not feel able to pursue the mathematical implications of a theory of multiplicities. He had, in fact, profoundly changed the

direction of the Riemannian distinction. Continuous multiplicities seemed to him to belong essentially to the sphere of duration. In this way, for Bergson, duration was not simply the indivisible, nor was it the nonmeasurable. Rather, it was that which divided only by changing in kind, that which was susceptible to measurement only by varying its metrical principle at each stage of the division. Bergson did not confine himself to opposing a philosophical vision of duration to a scientific conception of space but took the problem into the sphere of the two kinds of multiplicity. He thought that the multiplicity proper to duration had, for its part, a "precision" as great as that of science; moreover, that it should react upon science and open up a path for it that was not necessarily the same as that of Riemann and Einstein. This is why we must attach so much importance to the way in which Bergson, borrowing the notion of multiplicity, gives it renewed range and distribution.

How is the qualitative and continuous multiplicity of duration defined, in opposition to quantitative or numerical multiplicity? A difficult passage from *Time and Free Will* is particularly significant in this respect as it foreshadows the developments in *Matter and Memory*. It distinguishes the subjective and the objective: "We apply the term subjective to what seems to be completely and adequately known; and the term objective, to what is known in such a way that a constantly increasing number of new impressions could be substituted for the idea which we actually have of it."[5] If we confine ourselves to these formulations, we run the risk of misunderstandings, which are fortunately dispelled by the context. Bergson in fact specifies that an *object* can be divided up in an infinity of ways. Now, even before these divisions are made, they are grasped by thought as possible, without anything changing in the total aspect of the object. They are therefore already visible in the image of the object: Even when not realized (but simply possible), they are actually perceived, or at least perceptible in principle. "This actual, not merely virtual, apperception of subdivisions in the undivided is precisely what we call objectivity." Bergson means that the objective is *that which has no virtuality* — whether realized or not, whether possible or real, everything is actual in the objective. The first chapter of *Matter and Memory* develops this theme more clearly: Matter has neither virtuality nor hidden power, and that is why we can assimilate it to "the image." No doubt there can be *more* in matter than in the image we have of it, but there cannot be anything else in it, of a different kind.[6] And in another passage Bergson praises Berkeley for having assimilated body and idea, precisely because matter "has no interior, no underneath,...hides nothing, contains nothing...possesses neither power nor virtuality of any kind... is spread out as mere surface and...is no more than what it presents to us at any given moment."[7]

In short, "object" and "objective" denote not only what is divided, but what, in dividing, does not change in kind. It is thus what divides by differences in degree.[8] The object is characterized by the perfect equivalence of the divided and the divisions, of number and unit. In this sense, the object will be called a "numerical multiplicity." For number, and primarily the arithmetical unit itself, is the model of that which divides without changing in kind. This is the same as saying that number has only differences in degree, or that its differences, whether realized *or not*, are always actual in it. "The units by means of which arithmetic forms numbers are *provisional* units which can be subdivided without limit, and...each of them is the sum of fractional quantities, as small and as numerous as we like to imagine.... While all multiplication implies the possibility of treating any number whatever as a provisional unit that can be added to itself, conversely the units in their turn are true numbers which are as big as we like, but are regarded as provisionally indivisible for the purpose of compounding them with one another. Now, the very admission that it is possible to divide the unit into as many parts as we like, shows that we regard it as extended."9

On the other hand, what is a qualitative multiplicity? What is the subject or the subjective? Bergson gives the following example: "A complex feeling will contain a fairly large number of simple elements; but as long as these elements do not stand out with perfect clearness, we cannot say that they were completely realized, and as soon as consciousness has a distinct perception of them, the psychic state which results from their synthesis will have changed for this very reason."10 (For example, a complex of love and hatred is actualized in consciousness, but hatred and love become conscious under such conditions that they differ in kind from one another and also differ in kind from the unconscious complex). It would therefore be a serious mistake to think that duration was simply the indivisible, although for convenience, Bergson often expresses himself in this way. In reality, duration divides up and does so constantly: That is why it is a *multiplicity*. But it does not divide up without changing in kind, it changes in kind in the process of dividing up: This is why it is a nonnumerical multiplicity, where we can speak of "indivisibles" at each stage of the division. There is *other* without there being *several*; number exists only potentially.11 In other words, the subjective, or duration, is the *virtual*. To be more precise, it is the virtual insofar as it is actualized, in the course of being actualized, it

42

is inseparable from the movement of its actualization. For actualization comes about through differentiation, through divergent lines, and creates so many differences in kind by virtue of its own movement. Everything is actual in a numerical multiplicity; everything is not "realized," but everything there is actual. There are no relationships other than those between actuals, and no differences other than those in degree. On the other hand, a nonnumerical multiplicity by which duration or subjectivity is defined, plunges into another dimension, which is no longer spatial and is purely temporal: It moves from the virtual to its actualization, it actualizes itself by creating lines of differentiation that correspond to its differences in kind. A multiplicity of this kind has, essentially, the three properties of continuity, heterogeneity, and simplicity. In this instance Bergson does not have any real difficulty in reconciling heterogeneity and continuity.

The aforementioned passage from *Time and Free Will*, wherein Bergson distinguishes the subjective and the objective, appears to be all the more important insofar as it is the first to introduce indirectly the notion of the virtual. This notion of the virtual will come to play an increasingly important role in Bergsonian philosophy.[12] For, as we shall see, the same author who rejects the concept of *possibility* — reserving a use for it only in relation to matter and to closed systems, but always seeing it as the source of all kinds of false problems — is also he who develops the notion of the *virtual* to its highest degree and bases a whole philosophy of memory and life on it.

A very important aspect of the notion of multiplicity is the way in which it is distinguished from a theory of the One and the Multiple. The notion of multiplicity saves us from thinking in terms of "One and Multiple." There are many theories in philosophy that combine the one and the multiple. They share the characteristic of claiming to reconstruct the real with general ideas. We are told that the Self is one (thesis) and it is multiple (antithesis), then it is the unity of the multiple (synthesis). Or else we are told that the One is already multiple, that Being passes into nonbeing and produces becoming. The passages where Bergson condemns this movement of abstract thought are among the finest in his oeuvre. To Bergson, it seems that in this type of *dialectical* method, one begins with concepts that, like baggy clothes, are much too big.[13] The One in general, the multiple in general, nonbeing in general.... In such cases the real is recomposed with abstracts; but of what use is a dialectic that believes itself to be reunited with the real when it compensates for the inadequacy of a concept that is too broad or too general by invoking the opposite concept, which is no less broad and general? The concrete will never be attained by combining the inadequacy of one concept with the inadequacy of its opposite. The singular will never be attained by correcting a generality with another generality. In all this, Bergson clearly has in mind Hamelin whose *Essai sur les éléments principaux de la représentation* dates from 1907. Bergsonism's incompatibility with Hegelianism, indeed with any dialectical method, is also evident in these passages. Bergson criticizes the dialectic for being a *false movement*, that is, a movement of the abstract concept, which goes from one opposite to the other only by means of imprecision.[14]

Once again there is a Platonic tone in Bergson. Plato was the first to deride those who said "the One is multiple and the multiple one — Being is nonbeing," etc. In each case he asked *how, how many, when and where.* "What" unity of the multiple and "what" multiple of the one?[15] The combination of opposites tells us nothing; it forms a net so slack that everything slips through. Those metaphors of Plato about carving and the good cook (which Bergson likes so much) correspond to Bergson's invocation of the good tailor and the well-fitted outfit. This is what the precise concept must be like. "What really matters to philosophy is to know *what* unity, *what* multiplicity, *what reality* superior to the abstract one and the abstract multiple is the multiple unity of the person.... Concepts...ordinarily go by pairs and represent the two opposites. There is scarcely any concrete reality upon which one cannot take two opposing views at the same time and that is consequently not subsumed under the two antagonistic concepts. Hence a thesis and an antithesis which it would be vain for us to try logically to reconcile, for the simple reason that never, with concepts or points of view, will you make a thing.... If I try to *analyze* duration, that is, to resolve it into ready-made concepts, I am obliged by the very nature of the concept and the analysis to take two opposing views of *duration in general*, with which I shall then claim to recompose it. This combination can present neither a diversity of degrees nor a variety of forms: It is, or it is not. I shall say, for example, that there is, on the one hand, a *multiplicity* of successive states of consciousness and, on the other hand, a *unity* which binds them together. Duration will be the *synthesis* of this unity and multiplicity, but how this mysterious operation can admit of shades or degrees, I repeat, is not quite clear."[16]

What Bergson calls for – against the dialectic, against a general conception of opposites (the One and the Multiple) – is an acute perception of the "what" and the "how many," of what he calls the "nuance" or the potential number. Duration is opposed to becoming precisely because it is a multiplicity, a

45

type of multiplicity that is not reducible to an overly broad combination in which the opposites, the One and the Multiple in general, only coincide on condition that they are grasped at the extreme point of their generalization, empty of all "measure" and of all real substance. This multiplicity that is duration is not at all the same thing as the multiple, any more than its simplicity is the same as the One.

Two forms of the negative are often distinguished: The negative of simple limitation and the negative of opposition. We are assured that the substitution of the second form for the first by Kant and the post-Kantians was a revolution in philosophy. It is all the more remarkable that Bergson, in his critique of the negative, condemns both forms. Both seem to him to involve and to demonstrate the same inadequacy. For if we consider negative notions like *disorder* or *nonbeing*, their very conception (from the starting-point of being and order as the limit of a "deterioration" in whose interval all things are [analytically] included) amounts to the same thing as our conceiving of them in opposition to being and order, as forces that exercise power and combine with their opposites to produce (synthetically) all things. Bergson's critique is thus a double one insofar as it condemns, in both forms of the negative, the same ignorance of *differences in kind*, which are sometimes treated as "deteriorations," sometimes as oppositions. The heart of Bergson's project is to think differences in kind independently of all forms of negation: There are differences in being and yet nothing negative. Negation always involves abstract concepts that are much too general. What is, in fact, the common root of all negation? We have already seen it. Instead of starting out from a difference in kind between two orders, from a difference in kind between two beings, a general idea of order or

46

being is created, which can no longer be thought except in opposition to a nonbeing in general, a disorder in general, *or else* which can only be posited as the starting point of a deterioration that leads us to disorder in general or to nonbeing in general. In any case, the question of difference in kind — "what" order? "what" being? — has been neglected. Likewise the difference in kind between the two types of multiplicity has been neglected: Thus a general idea of the One is created and is combined with its opposite, the Multiple in general, to reconstruct all things from the standpoint of the force opposed to the multiple or to the deterioration of the One. In fact, it is the category of multiplicity, with the difference in kind between two types that it involves, which enables us to condemn the mystification of a thought that operates in terms of the One and the Multiple. We see, therefore, how all the critical aspects of Bergsonian philosophy are part of a single theme: a critique of the negative of limitation, of the negative of opposition, of general ideas.

*　　*　　*

"If we analyze in the same way the concept of motion...."[17] In fact, movement as physical experience is itself a composite: on the one hand, the space traversed by the moving object, which forms an indefinitely divisible numerical multiplicity, all of whose parts — real or possible — are actual and differ only in degree; on the other hand, pure movement, which is *alteration*, a virtual qualitative multiplicity, like the run of Achilles that is divisible into steps, but which changes qualitatively each time that it divides.[18] Bergson discovers that beneath the local transfer there is always a conveyance of another nature. And what seemed from outside to be a numerical part, a com-

47

ponent of the run, turns out to be, experienced from inside, an obstacle avoided.

But in doubling the psychological experience of duration with the physical experience of movement, one problem becomes pressing. The question "Do external things endure?" remained indeterminate from the standpoint of psychological experience. Moreover, in *Time and Free Will*, Bergson invoked on two occasions an "inexpressible," an "incomprehensible" reason — "What duration is there existing outside us? The present only, or, if we prefer the expression, simultaneity. No doubt external things change, but their moments do not *succeed* (in the ordinary sense of the word) one another, except for a consciousness that keeps them in mind.... Hence we must not say that external things *endure*, but rather that there is some inexpressible reason in them which accounts for our inability to examine them at successive moments of our own duration without observing that they have changed." — "Although things do not endure as we do ourselves, nevertheless, there must be some incomprehensible reason why phenomena are seen to *succeed* one another instead of being set out all at once."[19]

However, *Time and Free Will* already had an analysis of movement. But movement had been primarily posited as a "fact of consciousness" implying a conscious and enduring subject confused with duration as psychological experience. It is only to the extent that movement is grasped as belonging to things as much as to consciousness that it ceases to be confused with psychological duration, whose point of application it will displace, thereby necessitating that things participate directly in duration itself. If qualities exist in things no less than they do in consciousness, if there is a movement of qualities outside myself, things must, of necessity, endure in their own way. Psychological duration should be only a clearly determined case, an opening onto an ontological duration. Ontology should, of necessity, be possible. For duration was defined from the start as a multiplicity. Will this multiplicity not — thanks to movement — become confused with being itself? And, since it is endowed with very special properties, in what sense can it be said that there are *several* durations; in what sense can there be said to be a *single one*; in what sense can one get beyond the ontological alternative of one/several? A related problem now becomes more urgent. If things endure, or if there is duration in things, the question of space will need to be reassessed on new foundations. For space will no longer simply be a form of exteriority, a sort of screen that denatures duration, an impurity that comes to disturb the pure, a relative that is opposed to the absolute: Space itself will need to be based in things, in relations between things and between durations, to belong itself to the absolute, to have its own "purity." This was to be the double progression of the Bergsonian philosophy.

CHAPTER III

Memory as Virtual Coexistence

Duration is essentially memory, consciousness and freedom. It is consciousness and freedom because it is primarily memory. Now, Bergson always presents this identity of memory and duration in two ways: "the conservation *and* preservation of the past in the present." Or else "*whether* the present distinctly contains the ever-growing image of the past, or whether by its continual changing of quality attests rather to the increasingly heavy burden dragged along behind one the older one grows." Or again: "memory in these *two forms*, covering as it does with a cloak of recollections a core of immediate perception, and also contracting a number of external moments."[1] In fact we should express in two ways the manner in which duration is distinguished from a discontinuous series of instants repeated identically: On the one hand, "the following moment always contains, over and above the preceding one, the memory the latter has left it";[2] on the other hand, the two moments contract or condense into each other since one has not yet disappeared when another appears. There are, therefore, two memories — or two indissolubly linked aspects of memory—

recollection–memory and contraction–memory (If we ask what, in the final analysis, is the basis of this duality in duration, doubtless we find ourselves in a movement — which we shall examine later — by which the "present" that endures divides at each "instant" into two directions, one oriented and dilated toward the past, the other contracted, contracting toward the future).

But pure duration is itself the result of a division that is only operative "in principle" *(en droit)*. It is clear that memory is identical to duration, that it is coextensive with duration, but this proposition is valid in principle more than in fact. The special problem of memory is: How, by what mechanism, does duration become memory in fact? How does that which exists in principle actualize itself? In the same way, Bergson shows that consciousness is, in principle, coextensive with life; but how, and under what conditions, does life in fact become self-consciousness?[3]

*   *   *

Let us resume the analysis of the first chapter of *Matter and Memory*. We are led to distinguish five senses or aspects of subjectivity: (1) *need-subjectivity*, the moment of negation (need makes a hole in the continuity of things and holds back everything that interests it about the object, letting the rest go by); (2) *brain-subjectivity*, the moment of interval or of indetermination (the brain gives us the means of "choosing" that which corresponds to our needs in the object; introducing an interval between received and executed movement, it is itself the choice between two ways because, in itself, by virtue of its network of nerves, it divides up excitation infinitely and also because, in relation to the motor cells of the core it leaves us to choose between several possible reactions); (3) *affection-subjectivity*, the moment of pain (because affection is the price paid by the brain or by conscious perception; perception does not reflect possible action, nor does the brain bring about the interval without the assurance that certain organic parts are committed to the immobility of a purely receptive role that surrenders them to pain); (4) *recollection-subjectivity*, the primary aspect of memory (recollection being what comes to fill the interval, being embodied or actualized in the properly cerebral interval [*intervalle*]); (5) *contraction-subjectivity*, the second aspect of memory (the body being no more a punctiform instant in time than a mathematical point in space, and bringing about a contraction of the experienced excitations from which quality is born).

Now, these five aspects are not merely organized in order of increasing depth, but *are distributed on two very different lines of facts*. The first chapter of *Matter and Memory* sets out to decompose a composite (Representation) in two divergent directions: matter and memory, perception and recollection, objective and subjective (cf. the two multiplicities of *Time and Free Will*). Of the five aspects of subjectivity, the first two obviously belong to the objective line, since the first confines itself to abstracting from the object, and the second confines itself to establishing a zone of indetermination. The case of affection, the third sense, is more complex; it undoubtedly depends on the intersection of the two lines. But the positivity of affection, in its turn, is not yet the presence of a pure subjectivity that would be opposed to pure objectivity, it is rather the "impurity" that disturbs the latter.[4] The province of the pure line of subjectivity is thus the fourth, and then the fifth sense. Only the two aspects of memory strictly signify subjectivity, the other meanings confine themselves to making way for or bringing about the insertion of one line into the other, the intersection of one line with the other.

*   *   *

The question "Where are recollections preserved?" involves a false problem, that is to say, a badly analyzed composite. It is as though recollections had to be preserved somewhere, as though, for example, the brain were capable of preserving them. But the brain is wholly on the line of objectivity: There cannot be any difference in kind between the other states of matter and the brain. For in the latter everything is movement, as in the pure perception that it determines. (And yet the term *movement* obviously must not be understood in the sense of enduring movement, but on the contrary as an "instantaneous section.")[5] Recollection, on the contrary, is part of the line of subjectivity. It is absurd to mix the two lines by conceiving of the brain as the reservoir or the substratum of recollections. Moreover, an examination of the second line would be sufficient to show that recollections do not have to be preserved anywhere other than "in" duration. *Recollection therefore is preserved in itself.* Only then "did I become aware of the fact that inward experience in the pure state, in giving us a 'substance' whose very essence is to endure and consequently to prolong continually into the present an indestructible past, would have relieved me from seeking and would even have forbidden me to seek, where recollection is preserved. It preserves itself...."[6] Moreover, we have no interest in presupposing a preservation of the past elsewhere than *in itself*, for example, in the brain. The brain, in its turn, would need to have the power to preserve itself; we would need to confer this power of preservation that we have denied to duration on a state of matter, or even on the whole of matter.[7]

We are touching on one of the most profound, but perhaps also one of the least understood, aspects of Bergsonism: the theory of memory. There must be a difference in kind between matter and memory, between pure perception and pure recollection, between the present and the past, as there is between the two lines previously distinguished. We have great difficulty in understanding a survival of the past in itself because we believe that the past is no longer, that it has ceased to be. We have thus confused Being with being-present. Nevertheless, the present *is not*; rather, it is pure becoming, always outside itself. It *is* not, but it acts. Its proper element is not being but the active or the useful. The past, on the other hand, has ceased to act or to be useful. But it has not ceased to be. Useless and inactive, impassive, it IS, in the full sense of the word: It is identical with being in itself. It should not be said that it "was," since it is the in-itself of being, and the form under which being is preserved in itself (in opposition to the present, the form under which being is consummated and places itself outside of itself). At the limit, the ordinary determinations are reversed: of the present, we must say at every instant that it "was," and of the past, that it "is," that it is eternally, for all time. This is the difference in kind between the past and the present.[8] But this first aspect of the Bergsonian theory would lose all sense if its extra-psychological range were not emphasized. What Bergson calls "pure recollection" has no psychological existence. This is why it is called *virtual*, inactive, and unconscious. All these words are dangerous, in particular, the word "unconscious" which, since Freud, has become inseparable from an especially effective and active psychological existence. We will have occasion to compare the Freudian unconscious with the Bergsonian, since Bergson himself made the comparison.[9] We must nevertheless be clear at this point that Bergson does not use the word "unconscious" to denote a psychological reality outside consciousness, but to denote a nonpsychological reality — being as it is in itself. Strictly speaking, the psychological is the present. Only the present is "psychological"; but the past is pure ontology; pure recollection has only ontological significance.[10]

Let us now quote the admirable passage where Bergson summarizes the whole of his theory. When we look for a recollection that escapes us, "We become conscious of an act *sui generis* by which we detach ourselves from the present in order to replace ourselves, first in the past in general, then in a certain region of the past — a work of adjustment, something like the focusing of a camera. But our recollection still remains virtual; we simply prepare ourselves to receive it by adopting the appropriate attitude. Little by little it comes into view like a condensing cloud; from the virtual state it passes into the actual...."[11] Here again, one must avoid an overly psychological interpretation of the text. Bergson does indeed speak of a psychological act; but if this act is "*sui generis*," this is because it has made a genuine *leap*. We place ourselves *at once* in the past; we leap into the past as into a proper element.[12] In the same way that we do not perceive things in ourselves, but at the place where they are, we only grasp the past at the place where it is in itself, and not in ourselves, in our present. There is therefore a "past in general" that is not the particular past of a particular present but that is like an ontological element, a past that is eternal and for all time, the condition of the "passage" of every particular present. It is the past in general that makes possible all pasts. According to Bergson, we first put ourselves back into the past in general: He describes in this way the *leap into ontology*. We really leap into being, into being-in-itself, into the being in itself of the past. It is a case of leaving psychology altogether. It is a case of an immemorial or ontological Memory. It is only then, once the leap has been made, that recollection will gradually take on a psychological existence: "from the virtual it passes into the actual state...." We have had to search at the place where it is, in impassive Being, and gradually we give it an embodiment, a "psychologization."

The parallels between this text and some others must be emphasized. For Bergson analyzes language in the same way as memory. The way in which we understand what is said to us is identical to the way in which we find a recollection. Far from recomposing sense on the basis of sounds that are heard and associated images, we *place ourselves at once* in the element of sense, then in a region of this element. A true leap into Being. It is only then that sense is actualized in the psychologically perceived sounds, and in the images that are psychologically associated with the sounds. Here there is a kind of transcendance of sense and an ontological foundation of language that, as we shall see, are particularly important in the work of an author whose critique of language is considered to have been overly hasty.[13]

We must place ourselves at once in the past — in a leap, in a jump. Here again, this almost Kirkegaardian idea of a "leap" is strange in the work of a philosopher who is considered to be so attached to continuity. What does it mean? Bergson constantly says: You will never recompose the past with presents, no matter what they may be: "The image pure and simple will not take me back to the past unless, indeed, it was in the past that I sought it."[14] The past, it is true, seems to be caught between two presents: the old present that it once was and the actual present in relation to which it is now past. Two false beliefs are derived from this: On the one hand, we believe that the past as such is only constituted *after* having been present; on the other hand, that it is in some way reconstituted by the new present whose past it now is. This double illusion is at the heart of all physiological and psychological theories of memory. When one is influenced by such an illusion, one assumes that there is only a difference in degree between recollection and perception. We are thus entangled in a badly analyzed composite. This composite is the image as psychological reality. The image in effect retains something of the regions where we have had to look for the recollection that it actualizes or embodies. But it does not actualize this recollection without adapting it to the requirements of the present; it makes it into something of the present. Thus, we substitute the simple differences in degree between recollection-images and perception-images for the difference in kind between the present and the past, between pure perception and pure memory.

We are too accustomed to thinking in terms of the "present." We believe that a present is only past when it is replaced by another present. Nevertheless, let us stop and reflect for a moment: How would a new present come about if the old present did not pass at the same time that it *is* present? How would any present whatsoever pass, if it were not past *at the same time* as present? The past would never be constituted if it *had not been* constituted first of all, at the same time that it was present. There is here, as it were, a fundamental position of time and also the most profound paradox of memory: The past is "contemporaneous" with the present that it *has been*. If the past had to wait in order to be no longer, if it was not immediately and now that it had passed, "past in general," it could never become what it is, it would never be *that* past. If it were not constituted immediately, neither could it be reconstituted on the basis of an ulterior present. The past would never be constituted if it did not coexist with the present whose past it is.[15] The past and the present do not denote two successive moments, but two elements which coexist: One is the present, which does not cease to pass, and the other is the past, which does not cease to be but through which all presents pass. It is in this sense that there is a pure past, a kind of "past in general": The past does not follow the present, but on the contrary, is presupposed by it as the pure condition without which it would not pass. In other words, each present goes back to itself as past. The only equivalent thesis is Plato's notion of Reminiscence. The reminiscence also affirms a pure being of the past, a being in itself of the past, an ontological Memory that is capable of serving as the foundation for the unfolding of time. Yet again, a Platonic inspiration makes itself profoundly felt in Bergson.[16]

The idea of a contemporaneity of the present and the past has one final consequence: Not only does the past coexist with the present that has been, but, as it preserves itself in itself (while the present passes), it is the whole, integral past; it is *all* our past, which coexists with each present. The famous metaphor of the cone represents this complete state of coexistence. But such a state implies, finally, that in the past itself there appear all kinds of levels of profundity, marking all the possible intervals in this coexistence.[17] The past AB coexists with the present S, but by including in itself all the sections A'B', A"B", etc., that measure the degrees of a purely ideal

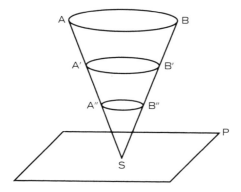

proximity or distance in relation to S. Each of these sections is itself *virtual*, belonging to the being in itself of the past.[18] Each of these sections or each of these levels includes not particular elements of the past, but always the totality of the past. It includes this totality at a more or less expanded or contracted level. This is the precise point at which contraction-Memory fits in with recollection-Memory and, in a way, *takes over from it*. Hence this consequence: Bergsonian duration is, in the final analysis, defined less by succession than by coexistence.

In *Time and Free Will* duration is really defined by succession, coexistences referring back to space, and by the power of novelty, repetition referring back to Matter. But, more profoundly, duration is only succession relatively speaking (we have seen in the same way that it is only indivisible relatively). Duration is indeed real succession, but it is so only because, more profoundly, it is *virtual coexistence*: the coexistence with itself of all the levels, all the tensions, all the degrees of contraction and relaxation (*détente*). Thus, with coexistence, repetition must be reintroduced into duration – a "psychic" repetition of a completely different type than the "physical" repetition of matter; a repetition of "planes" rather than of elements on a single plane; virtual instead of actual repetition. The whole of our past is played, restarts, repeats itself, *at the same time*, on all the levels that it sketches out.[19] Let us return to the "leap" that we make when, looking for a recollection, we place ourselves at once in the past. Bergson gives the following clarification: We place ourselves "firstly into the past in general, then into a certain region of the past." It is not a case of one region containing particular elements of the past, particular recollections, in opposition to another region which contains other recollections. It is a case of there being distinct levels, each one of which contains the whole of our past, but in a more or less contracted state. It is in this sense that one can speak of the regions of Being itself, the ontological regions of the past "in general," all coexisting, all "repeating" one another.

Later we shall see how this doctrine revives all the problems of Bergsonism. However, at this point it is enough to summarize the four main propositions that form as many paradoxes: (1) we place ourselves at once, in a leap, in the ontological element of the past (paradox of the leap); (2) there is a difference in kind between the present and the past (paradox of Being); (3) the past does not follow the present that it has been, but coexists with it (paradox of coexistence); (4) what coexists with each present is the whole of the past, integrally, on various levels of contraction and relaxation (*détente*) (paradox of psychic repetition). These paradoxes are interconnected; each one is dependent on the others. Conversely, the propositions that they attack also form a group, insofar as these propositions are characterized by their being ordinary theories of memory. For it is a single illusion about the essence of Time, a single badly analyzed composite that makes us believe that: (1) we can reconstitute the past with the present; (2) we pass gradually from one to the other; (3) that they are distinguished by a before and an after; and (4) that the work of the mind is carried out by the addition of elements (rather than by changes of level, genuine jumps, the reworking of systems).[20]

*　*　*

Our problem is: How can pure recollection take on a psychological existence? How will this pure virtual be actualized? Thus the present makes an appeal, according to the requirements or needs of the present situation. We make the "leap": We place ourselves not simply in the element of the past in general, but in a particular region, that is, on a particular level which, in a kind of Reminiscence, we assume corresponds to our actual needs. Each level in effect contains the totality of our past, but in a more or less contracted state. And Bergson adds: There are also dominant recollections, like *remarkable points*, which vary from one level to the other.[21] A foreign word is spoken in my presence: Given the situation this is not the same thing as wondering what the language in general, of which this word is a part, could be or what person once said this word, or a similar one, to me. Depending on the case, I do not leap into the same region of the past; I do not place myself on the same level; I do not appeal to the same essential characteristics. Perhaps I fail: Looking for a recollection, I may place myself on a level that is too contracted, too narrow, or on the contrary, too broad and expanded for it. I would then have to start from the beginning again in order to find the correct leap. We must emphasize that this analysis, which seems to have so much psychological finesse, really has a quite different meaning. It is related to our affinity with being, our relationship with Being,

and to the variety of this relationship. Psychological consciousness has not yet been born. It will be born, but precisely
because it has found its proper ontological conditions here.

Faced with these extremely difficult texts, the task of the
commentator is to multiply the distinctions, even and above
all when these texts confine themselves to suggesting the distinctions, rather than to establishing them strictly. First, we
must not confuse the appeal to recollection and the "recall of
the image" (or its evocation). The appeal to recollection is this
jump by which I place myself in the virtual, in the past, in a
particular region of the past, at a particular level of contraction. It appears that this appeal expresses the properly ontological dimension of man or, rather, of memory: "But our
recollection still remains virtual."[22] When, on the other hand,
we speak of evocation, or of this recall of the image, something completely different is involved: Once we have put ourselves on a particular level where recollections lie, then, and
only then, do they tend to be actualized. The appeal of the
present is such that they no longer have the ineffectiveness,
the impassivity that characterized them as pure recollections;
they become recollection-images, capable of being "recalled."
They are actualized or embodied. This actualization has all kinds
of distinct aspects, stages, and degrees.[23] But through these
stages and these degrees it is the actualization (and it alone)
that constitutes psychological consciousness. In any case, the
Bergsonian revolution is clear: We do not move from the present to the past, from perception to recollection, but from the
past to the present, from recollection to perception.

"Memory, laden with the whole of the past, responds to the
appeal of the present state by two simultaneous movements,
one of *translation*, by which it moves in its entirety to meet expe-

rience, thus *contracting* more or less, though without dividing, with a view to action; the other of *rotation* upon itself, by which it *turns toward* the situation of the moment, presenting to it that side of itself which may prove to be the most useful."[24] Thus we already have two aspects of actualization here: translation–contraction and rotation–orientation. Our question is: Can this translation–contraction be identical with the variable contraction of regions and levels of the past that we were discussing earlier? Bergson's context seems to suggest that it is, since he constantly invokes translation–contraction with regard to sections of the cone, that is, levels of the past.[25] Many considerations, however, lead us to the conclusion that while there is obviously a relationship between the two contractions, they are by no means identical. When Bergson speaks of levels or regions of the past, these levels are no less virtual than the past in general; moreover, each one of them contains the whole of the past, but in a more or less contracted state, around certain variable dominant recollections. The extent of the contraction, therefore, expresses the difference between one level and another. On the other hand, when Bergson speaks of translation, it involves a movement that is necessary in the actualization of a recollection taken from a particular level. Here contraction no longer expresses the ontological difference between two virtual levels, but the movement by which a recollection is (psychologically) actualized, *at the same time* as the level that belongs to it.[26]

It would, in fact, be a mistake to think that, in order to be actualized, a recollection must pass through more and more contracted levels in order to approach the present as the supreme point of contraction or the summit of the cone. This would be an untenable interpretation for several reasons. In the metaphor of the cone, even a level that is very contracted, very close to the summit — so long as it is not actualized — displays a genuine difference in kind from this summit, that is, from the present. Furthermore, in order to actualize a recollection, we do not have to change levels; if we had to do this, the operation of memory would be impossible. For each recollection has its own proper level; it is too dismembered or dispersed in broader regions, too confined and muddled in narrower regions. If we had to pass from one level to another in order to actualize each recollection, each recollection would thus lose its individuality. This is why the movement of translation is a movement by which the recollection is actualized at the same time as its level: There is contraction because recollection-becoming-image enters into a "coalescence" with the present. It therefore passes through "planes of consciousness" that put it into effect. But it does *not* pass through the intermediate levels (which would prevent it from being put into effect). Hence the need to avoid confusing the *planes of consciousness*, through which recollection is actualized, and *the regions, the sections or the levels of the past*, according to which the always virtual state of recollection varies. Hence the need to distinguish intensive, ontological contraction — where all the levels coexist virtually, contracted or relaxed (*détendus*) — and translative, psychological contraction through which each recollection on its own level (however relaxed [*détendu*] it is) must pass in order to be actualized and thereby become image.

But, on the other hand, Bergson says, there is rotation. In its process of actualization, recollection does not confine itself to carrying out this translation that unites it to the present; it also carries out this rotation on itself in order to present its "useful facet" in this union. Bergson does not clarify the nature of this rotation. We must make hypotheses on the basis of other texts. In the movement of translation, it is therefore a whole level of the past that is actualized at the same time as a particular recollection. Each level thus finds itself contracted in an undivided representation that is no longer a pure recollection, but is not yet, strictly speaking, an image. This is why Bergson specifies that, from this point of view, there is no division at this point.[27] Recollection undoubtedly has its individuality. But how do we become conscious of it, how do we distinguish it in the region that is actualized with it? We begin from this undivided representation (that Bergson will call "dynamic scheme"), where all the recollections in the process of actualization are in a relationship of reciprocal penetration; and we develop it in distinct images that are external to one another, that correspond to a particular recollection.[28] Here again, Bergson speaks of a succession of "planes of consciousness." But the movement is no longer that of an undivided contraction. It is, on the contrary, that of a division, a development, an expansion. Recollection can only be said to be actualized when it has become image. It is then, in fact, that it enters not only into "coalescence," but into a kind of *circuit* with the present, the recollection-image referring back to the perception-image and vice versa.[29] Hence the preceding metaphor of "rotation" which prepares the ground for this launch into the circuit.

Thus, we have here two movements of actualization: one of contraction, one of expansion. We can see clearly that they correspond closely to the multiple levels of the cone, some expanded (*détendus*), some contracted. For what happens in a creature that confines itself to dreaming? Since sleep is like a present situation requiring nothing but rest, with no interest other than "disinterest," it is as if the contraction were missing, as if the extremely expanded (*détendu*) relationship of the recollection with the present reproduced the most expanded (*détendu*) level of the past itself. Conversely, what would happen in an automaton? It would be as though dispersion were impossible, as though the distinction between images was no longer carried into effect and only the most contracted level of the past remained.[30] There is thus a close analogy between the different levels of the cone and the aspects of actualization for each level. *It is inevitable that the latter will come to include the former* (hence the ambiguity that has already been pointed out). Nevertheless, we must not confuse them because the first theme concerns the virtual variations of recollection in itself; the other, recollection for us, the actualization of the recollection in the recollection-image.

What is the framework common to recollection in the process of actualization (the recollection-becoming-image) and the perception-image? This common framework is movement. Thus, it is in the relationship between the image and movement, in the image's way of extending itself in movement, that we must find the final moments of actualization: "the recollections need, for their actualization, a motor ally."[31] Here again, the ally is double. Sometimes perception is extended naturally in movement; a motor tendency, a *motor scheme*, carries out a decomposition of the perceived in terms of utility.[32] This movement–perception relationship would, on its own, be sufficient to define a recognition that is purely automatic, without the intervention of recollections (or, if you prefer, an instantaneous memory consisting entirely in motor mechanisms). However, recollections *do* intervene. For, insofar as recollection-images resemble actual perception, they are necessarily extended into the movements that correspond to perception and they become "adopted" by it.[33]

Let us assume for a moment that a disturbance arises in this movement–perception–articulation, a *mechanical disturbance* of the motor scheme: Recognition has become impossible (although another type of recognition subsists, as we see in those patients who clearly describe an object that is named to them, but who do not know how to "make use" of it; or who correctly repeat what is said to them, but no longer know how to speak spontaneously). The patient no longer knows how to orient himself, how to draw, that is, how to decompose an object according to the motor tendencies: His perception only provokes diffuse movements. Nevertheless, the recollections are there. Moreover, they continue to be evoked, to be embodied in distinct images, that is, to undergo the translation and rotation that characterize the first moments of actualization. What is lacking therefore is the final moment, the final *phase*: that of action. Just as the concomitant movements of perception are disorganized, the recollection-image also remains as useless, as ineffective as a pure recollection, and can no longer extend itself into action. This is the first important fact: There are cases where recollections survive despite psychic or verbal blindness or deafness.[34]

Let us move on to the second type of movement–perception relationship that defines the conditions of an attentive recognition. It is no longer a matter of movements that "extend our perception in order to draw useful effects from it" and that decompose the object according to our needs, but of movements that abandon the effect, that *bring us back* to the object in order to restore its detail and completeness. Then the recollection-images — which are analogous to present perception —

take on a role that is "preponderant and no longer merely accessory," regular and no longer accidental.[35] Let us assume that this second kind of movement is disturbed (disturbance of the sensory motor functions that is *dynamic*, and no longer *mechanical*).[36] It is possible for automatic recognition to remain, but what does appear to have disappeared is recollection itself. Because such cases are the most frequent they have inspired the traditional conception of aphasia as the disappearance of recollections stored in the brain. Bergson's whole problem is: What has really disappeared?

First hypothesis: Is it pure recollection? Obviously not, since pure recollection is not psychological in nature and is imperishable. Second hypothesis: Is it the capacity to evoke recollection, that is, to actualize it in a recollection-image? At times, Bergson *does* express himself in this way.[37] Nevertheless, it is more complicated than this. For the first two aspects of actualization (translation and rotation) depend on a psychic attitude; the last two (the two types of movement) depend on sensory-motricity and the attitudes of bodies. Whatever the solidarity and complementarity of these two dimensions, the one cannot completely cancel out the other. When only the automatic movements of recognition are affected (mechanical disturbances of sensory-motricity), recollection nevertheless completely retains its psychic actualization; it preserves its "normal aspect," but can no longer extend itself in movement, the corporeal stage of its actualization having become impossible. When the movements of attentive recognition are affected (dynamic disturbances of sensory-motricity), psychical actualization is undoubtedly more endangered than in the preceding case for here the corporeal attitude really is a condition of the mental attitude. Bergson nevertheless maintains that, once again, no recollection is "inattentive." There is merely a "disturbance of the equilibrium."[38] We must perhaps understand that the two psychic aspects of actualization subsist but are, as it were, dissociated for want of a corporeal attitude in which they could be inserted and combined. Sometimes then, translation–contraction would occur, but would lack the complementary movement of rotation, so that there would be no distinct recollection-image (or, at least, a whole category of recollection-images would seem to have been abolished). Sometimes, on the contrary, rotation would occur, distinct images would form, but they would be detached from memory and abandon their solidarity with the others. In any case, it is not sufficient to say that, according to Bergson, pure recollection always preserves itself; we must add that illness never abolishes the recollection-image as such, but merely impairs a particular *aspect* of its actualization.

These, therefore, are the four aspects of actualization: translation and rotation, which form the properly psychic moments; dynamic movement, the attitude of the body that is necessary to the stable equilibrium of the two preceding determinations; and finally, mechanical movement, the motor scheme that represents the final stage of actualization. All this involves the adaptation of the past to the present, the utilization of the past in terms of the present – what Bergson calls "attention to life." The first moment ensures a point of contact between the past and the present: The past literally moves toward the present in order to find a point of contact (or of contraction) with it. The second moment ensures a transposition, a translation, an expansion of the past in the present: Recollection-images restore the distinctions of the past in the present – at least those that are useful. The third moment, the dynamic attitude of the body, ensures the harmony of the two preceding moments, correcting the one by the other and pushing them to their limit. The fourth moment, the mechanical movement of the body, ensures the proper utility of the whole and its performance in the present. But this utility, this performance, would be nothing if the four moments were not connected with a condition that is valid for them all. We have seen that pure recollection was contemporaneous with the present that it *had been*. Recollection, in the course of actualizing itself, thus tends to be actualized in an image that is itself contemporaneous to this present. Now it is obvious that such a recollection-image, such a "recollection of the present," would be completely useless since it would simply result in doubling the perception-image. Recollection must be embodied, not in terms of its own present (with which it is contemporaneous), but in terms of a new present, in relation to which it is now past. This condition is normally realized by the very nature of the present, which constantly passes by, moving forward and hollowing out an interval. This is therefore the fifth aspect of actualization: a kind of displacement by which the past is embodied only in terms of a present that is different from that which it has been. (The disturbance corresponding to this last aspect would be *paramnesia*, in which the "recollection of the present" would be actualized as such.)[39]

*   *   *

In this way a psychological unconscious, distinct from the ontological unconscious, is defined. The latter corresponds to a recollection that is pure, virtual, impassive, inactive, *in itself*. The former represents the movement of recollection in the course of actualizing itself: Like Leibnizian possibles, recollections try

71

to become embodied, they exert pressure to be admitted so that a full-scale repression originating in the present and an "attention to life" are necessary to ward off useless or dangerous recollections.[40] There is no contradiction between these two descriptions of two distinct unconsciousnesses. Moreover, the whole of *Matter and Memory* plays between the two, with consequences that we shall analyze later.

CHAPTER IV

One or Many Durations?

Thus far, the Bergsonian method has shown two main aspects, the one dualist, the other monist. First, the diverging lines or the differences in kind had to be followed beyond the "turn in experience"; then, still further beyond, the point of convergence of these lines had to be rediscovered, and the rights of a new monism restored.[1] This program is in fact realized in *Matter and Memory*. First, we bring out the difference in kind between the two lines of object and subject: between perception and recollection, matter and memory, present and past. What happens then? It certainly seems that when the recollection is actualized, its difference in kind from perception tends to be obliterated: There are no longer, there can no longer be, anything but differences in degree between recollection-images and perception-images.[2] It is for this reason that, without the method of intuition, we inevitably remain prisoners of a badly analyzed psychological composite whose original differences in kind we are unable to discern.

But it is clear that, at this level, a genuine point of unity is not yet available. The point of unity must account for a composite *from the other side* of the turn in experience; it must not be confused with the one in experience. And in fact, Bergson is not content to say that there are now only differences in degree between the recollection-image and the perception-image. He also presents a much more important ontological proposition: *While the past coexists with its own present, and while it coexists with itself on various levels of contraction, we must recognize that the present itself is only the most contracted level of the past.* This time it is pure present and pure past, pure perception and pure recollection as such, pure matter and pure memory that now have only differences of expansion (*détente*) and contraction and thus rediscover an ontological unity. But discovering a deeper contraction–memory at the heart of recollection-memory we have thus laid the foundations for the possibility of a new *monism*. At each instant, our perception contracts "an incalculable multitude of rememorized elements"; at each instant, our present infinitely contracts our past: "The two terms which had been separated to begin with cohere closely together...."[3] What, in fact, is a sensation? It is the operation of contracting trillions of vibrations onto a receptive surface. Quality emerges from this, quality that is nothing other than contracted quantity. This is how the notion of contraction (or of tension) allows us to go beyond the duality of homogeneous quantity and heterogeneous quality, and to pass from one to the other in a continuous movement. But, conversely, if our present, through which we place ourselves inside matter, is the most contracted degree of our past, matter itself will be like an infinitely dilated or relaxed (*détendu*) past (so relaxed that the preceding moment has disappeared when the following appears). This is how the idea of relaxation (*détente*) – or of extension – will overcome the duality of the unextended and the extended and give us the means of passing from one to the other. For perception itself is extensity, sensation is extensive insofar as what it contracts is precisely the extended, the expanded (*détendu*). (It makes space available to us "in the exact proportion" in which we have time available).[4]

Hence, the importance of *Matter and Memory*: Movement is attributed to things themselves so that material things partake directly of duration, and thereby form a limit case of duration. *The immediate data (les donées immédiates)* are surpassed: Movement is no less outside me than in me; and the Self itself in turn is only one case among others in duration.[5] But then all kinds of problems arise. Let us single out two important ones.

(1) Is there not a contradiction between the two moments of the method, between the dualism of differences in kind and the monism of contraction–relaxation (*détente*)? For, in the name of the first, philosophies that confine themselves to differences of *degree*, of *intensity* were condemned. Moreover, what were condemned were the false notions of degree, of intensity, as notions of contrariety or negation, sources of all false problems. Isn't Bergson now in the process of restoring all that he once dismissed? What differences can there be between relaxation (*détente*) and contraction except for the differences of degree, of intensity? The present is only the most contracted degree of the past, matter the most relaxed (*détendu*) degree of the present (*mens momentanea*).[6] And if we seek to correct what is too "gradual" here, we can only do so by reintroducing into duration all the contrariety, all the opposition that Bergson had previously condemned as so many abstract and inadequate conceptions. We will only escape from matter as deterioration of duration by embracing a conception of matter that is a "reversal" of duration.[7] What then becomes of the Bergsonian project of showing that Difference, as difference

in kind, could and should be understood independently of the *negative* (the negative of deterioration as well as the negative of opposition)? The worst contradiction of all seems to be set up at the heart of the system. Everything is reintroduced: degrees, intensity, opposition.

(2) Even supposing that this problem is solved, can we speak of a rediscovered monism? In one sense, yes, insofar as everything is duration. But, since duration is dissipated in all these differences in degree, intensity, relaxation (*détente*), and contraction that affect it, we tend instead to fall into a kind of quantitative pluralism. Hence, the importance of the following question: Is duration one or many, and in what sense? Have we really overcome dualism, or have we been engulfed in pluralism? We must begin with this question.

*   *   *

Bergson's texts seem to vary considerably on this point. *Matter and Memory* goes furthest in the affirmation of a radical plurality of durations: The universe is made up of modifications, disturbances, changes of tension and of energy, and nothing else. Bergson does indeed speak of a plurality of *rhythms* of duration; but in this context he makes it clear — in relation to durations that are more or less slow or fast — that each duration is an absolute, and that each rhythm is itself a duration.[8] In a key text from 1903, he insists on the progress made since *Time and Free Will*: Psychological duration, our duration, is now only one case among others, among an infinity of others, "a certain well-defined *tension*, whose very definitiveness seems like a choice between an infinity of possible durations."[9] We can see that, as in *Matter and Memory*, psychology is now only an opening onto ontology, a springboard for an "installation" in Being.

76

But no sooner are we installed, than we perceive that Being is multiple, the very numerous duration, our own, caught between more dispersed durations and more taut (*tendue*), more intense durations: "This being so one perceives any number of durations, all very different from one another...." The idea of a virtual coexistence of all the levels of the past, of all the levels of tension, is thus extended to the whole of the universe: This idea no longer simply signifies my relationship with being, but the relationship of all things with being. Everything happens as if the universe were a tremendous Memory. And Bergson is pleased with the power of the method of intuition: It alone enables us "to go beyond idealism as well as realism, to affirm the existence of objects which are *inferior* and *superior* to ourselves, although still, in a certain sense, internal to us, to make them *coexist* together without difficulty." This extension of virtual coexistence to an infinity of specific durations stands out clearly in *Creative Evolution*, where life itself is compared to a memory, the genera or species corresponding to coexisting degrees of this vital memory.[10] Thus we have an ontological vision that seems to imply a generalized pluralism. But it is precisely in *Creative Evolution* that a major limitation is underlined: If things are said to endure, it is less in themselves or absolutely than in relation to the Whole of the universe in which they participate insofar as their distinctions are artificial. Thus, the piece of sugar only makes us wait because, in spite of its arbitrary carving out, it opens out onto the universe as a whole. In this sense, each thing no longer has its own duration. The only ones that do are the beings similar to us (psychological duration), then the living beings that naturally form relative closed systems, and finally, the Whole of the universe.[11] It is thus a limited, not a generalized, pluralism.

Finally, *Duration and Simultaneity* recapitulates all the possible hypotheses: generalized pluralism, limited pluralism, monism.[12] According to the first, there is a coexistence of completely different rhythms, of durations that are really distinct, hence a radical multiplicity of Time. Bergson adds that he once advanced this hypothesis, but considered that apart from ourselves it was valid only for living species: "We did not see then, we still see today, no reason to extend this hypothesis of a multiplicity of durations to the material universe." Hence, a second hypothesis: Material things outside us would not be distinguished by absolutely different durations but by a certain relative way of participating in our duration and of giving it emphasis. Here it seems that Bergson is condensing the provisional doctrine of *Time and Free Will* (there is, as it were, a mysterious participation of things in our duration, an "inexpressible ground") and the more developed doctrine of *Creative Evolution* (this participation in our duration would be explained by things belonging to the Whole of the universe). But even in this second case, the mystery about the nature of the Whole and our relationship with it remains. Hence, the third hypothesis: There is only a single time, a single duration, in which everything would participate, including our consciousnesses, including living beings, including the whole material world. Now, to the reader's surprise, it is this hypothesis that Bergson puts forward as the most satisfactory: *a single Time, one, universal, impersonal.*[13] In short, a monism of Time.... Nothing could be more surprising; one of the other two hypotheses would seem to be a better expression of the state of Bergsonism, whether after *Matter and Memory* or after *Creative Evolution*. What is more: Has Bergson forgotten that in *Time and Free Will* he defined duration, that is real time, as a "multiplicity"?

What has happened? Undoubtedly the confrontation with the theory of Relativity. This confrontation was forced on Bergson because Relativity, for its part, invoked concepts such as expansion, contraction, tension and dilation in relation to space and time. But this confrontation did not come about suddenly: It was prepared by the fundamental notion of Multiplicity, which Einstein drew from Riemann, and which Bergson for his part had used in *Time and Free Will*. Let us recall, briefly, the principal characteristics of Einstein's theory, as Bergson summarizes them: Everything begins from a certain idea of movement that entails a contraction of bodies and a dilation of their time. From this we conclude that there has been a dislocation of simultaneity: What is simultaneous in a fixed system ceases to be simultaneous in a mobile system. Moreover, by virtue of the relativity of rest and movement, by virtue of the relativity even of accelerated movement, these contractions of extensity, these dilations of time, these ruptures of simultaneity become absolutely reciprocal. In this sense there would be a multiplicity of times, a plurality of times, with different speeds of flow, all real, each one peculiar to a system of reference. And as it becomes necessary, in order to situate a point, to indicate its position in time as well as in space, the only unity of time is in a fourth dimension of space. It is precisely this Space–Time bloc that actually divides up into space and into time in an infinity of ways, each one peculiar to a system.

To what does the discussion relate? Contraction, dilation, relativity of movement, multiplicity — all these notions are familiar to Bergson. He uses them for his own purposes. Bergson never gives up the idea that duration, that is to say time, is essentially multiplicity. But the problem is: What type of multiplicity? Remember that Bergson opposed two types of

79

multiplicity – actual multiplicities that are numerical and discontinuous and virtual multiplicities that are continuous and qualitative. It is clear that in Bergson's terminology, Einstein's Time belongs to the first category. Bergson criticizes Einstein for having confused the two types of multiplicity and for having, as a result, revived the confusion of time with space. The discussion only apparently deals with the question: Is time one or multiple? The true problem is "What is the multiplicity peculiar to time?" This clearly surfaces in Bergson's upholding of the existence of a single, universal and impersonal Time.

"When we are sitting on the bank of a river, the flowing of the water, the gliding of a boat or the flight of a bird, the uninterrupted murmur of our deep life, are for us three different things or a single one, at will...."[14] Here Bergson endows attention with the power of "apportioning without dividing," "of being one and several"; but more profoundly, he endows duration with the power to encompass itself. The flowing of the water, the flight of the bird, the murmur of my life form three fluxes; but only because my duration is one of them, and also the element that contains the two others. Why not make do with two fluxes, my duration and the flight of the bird, for example? Because the two fluxes could never be said to be coexistent or simultaneous if they were not contained in a third one. The flight of the bird and my own duration are only simultaneous insofar as my own duration divides in two and is reflected in another that contains it at the same time as it contains the flight of the bird: There is therefore a fundamental triplicity of fluxes.[15] It is in this sense that my duration essentially has the power to disclose other durations, to encompass the others, and to encompass itself ad infinitum. But we see that this infinity of reflection or attention gives duration back its true char-

acteristics, which must be constantly recalled: It is not simply
the indivisible, but that which has a very special style of division; it is not simply succession but a very special coexistence,
a simultaneity of fluxes. "Such is our first idea of simultaneity. We call simultaneous, then, two external fluxes that occupy
the same duration because they hold each other in the duration of a third, our own.... [It is this] simultaneity of fluxes
that brings us back to internal duration, to real duration."[16]

Let us return to the characteristics by which Bergson defines
duration as virtual or continuous multiplicity. On the one
hand, it divides into elements that differ in kind; on the other,
these elements or these parts only actually exist insofar as the
division itself is effectively carried out (If our consciousness
"terminates the division at a given point, there also terminates
divisibility.").[17] If we take up a position where the division has
not yet been carried out, that is, in the virtual, it is obvious
that there is only a single time. Then, let us take up another
position at a moment where the division has been carried out:
two fluxes, for example, that of Achilles' race and that of the
tortoise's race. We say that they differ in kind (as do each step
of Achilles and each step of the tortoise, if we take the division still further). The fact that the division is subject to the
condition of actually being carried out means that the parts
(fluxes) must be lived or at least posited and thought of as capable of being lived. Now Bergson's whole thesis *consists in dem-
onstrating that they can only be livable or lived in the perspective of a
single time*. The principle of the demonstration is as follows:
When we admit the existence of several times, we are not content to consider flux A and flux B or even the image that the
subject of A has of B (Achilles as he conceives or imagines the
tortoise's race as capable of being lived by the tortoise). In

order to posit the existence of two times, we are forced to introduce a strange factor: the image that A has of B, while nevertheless knowing that B cannot live in this way. This factor is completely "symbolic"; in other words, it opposes and excludes the lived experience and through it (and only it) is the so-called second time realized. From this Bergson concludes that there exists one Time and one Time only, as much on the level of the actual parts as on the level of the virtual Whole. (But what is the significance of this obscure demonstration? We shall soon see.)

If we follow the division in the other direction, if we go back, we see the fluxes each time *with their differences in kind, with their differences of contraction and expansion (détente)*, communicating in a single and identical Time, which is, as it were, their condition: "A single duration will pick up along its route the events of the totality of the material world; and we will then be able to eliminate the human consciousness that we had initially had available, every now and then, as so many relays for the movement of our thought: there will now only be impersonal time in which all things will flow."[18] Hence the triplicity of fluxes, our duration (the duration of a spectator) being necessary both as flux and as representative of Time in which all fluxes are engulfed. It is in this sense that Bergson's various texts are perfectly reconcilable and contain no contradiction: There is only one time (monism), although there is an infinity of actual fluxes (generalized pluralism) that necessarily participate in the same virtual whole (limited pluralism). Bergson in no way gives up the idea of a difference in kind between actual fluxes; any more than he gives up the idea of differences of relaxation (*détente*) or contraction in the virtuality that encompasses them and is actualized in them. But he considers that these two certainties do not exclude, but on the contrary imply, a single time. In short: Not only do virtual multiplicities imply a single time, but duration as virtual multiplicity is this single and same Time.

It is nonetheless true that the Bergsonian demonstration of the contradictory character of the plurality of times seems obscure. Let us clarify it at the level of the theory of Relativity. For, paradoxically, only this theory makes it appear clear and convincing. Insofar as we are dealing with qualitatively distinct fluxes, it may in fact be difficult to know whether or not the two subjects live and perceive the same time: We support unity, but only as the most "plausible" idea. On the other hand, the theory of Relativity is based on the following hypothesis: There are no longer qualitative fluxes, but systems, "in a state of reciprocal and uniform replacement" where the observers are interchangeable, since there is no longer a privileged system.[19] Let us accept this hypothesis. Einstein says that the time of the two systems, S and S', is not the same. But what is this *other* time? It is not that of Peter in S, nor that of Paul in S', since, by hypothesis, these two times only differ quantitatively, and this difference is cancelled out when one takes S and S' as systems of reference in turn. Could it at least be said that this other time is the one that Peter conceives as lived or capable of being lived by Paul? Not at all — *and this is the essential point of the Bergsonian argument.* "Undoubtedly Peter sticks a label on this Time in the name of Paul; but if he imagined Paul conscious, living his own duration and measuring it, for this very reason he would see Paul take his own system as a system of reference, and then place himself in this single Time, internal to each system, which we have just been speaking of: moreover, also for this very reason, Peter would provisionally surrender his system of reference and in consequence his existence as physicist, and in consequence also his consciousness; Peter would now only see himself as a vision of Paul."[20] In short, the *other* time is something that can neither be lived by Peter nor by Paul, nor by Paul as Peter imagines him. It is a pure symbol excluding the lived and indicating simply that such a system, and not the other, is taken as a reference point. "Peter no longer envisages Paul as a physicist, nor even a conscious being, nor even a being: he empties from his conscious and living interior the visual image of Paul, only retaining the external envelope of the character."

Thus, in the Relativity hypothesis, it becomes obvious that there can only be a single livable and lived time. (This demonstration goes beyond the relativist hypothesis, since qualitative differences, in their turn, cannot constitute numerical distinctions.) This is why Bergson claims that Relativity in fact demonstrates the opposite of what it asserts about the plurality of time.[21] All Bergson's other criticisms derive from this. For what simultaneity does Einstein have in mind when he states that it varies from one system to the other? A simultaneity defined by the readings of two distant clocks. And it is true that this simultaneity is variable or relative. But precisely because its relativity expresses, not something lived or livable, but the symbolic factor of which we have just been speaking.[22] In this sense, this simultaneity presupposes two others linked in the instant, simultaneities that are not variable but absolute: the simultaneity between two instants, taken from external movements (a nearby phenomenon and a moment of the clock), and the simultaneity of these instants with the instants taken by them from our duration. And these two simultaneities presuppose yet another, that of the fluxes, which is even less variable.[23] The Bergsonian theory of *simultaneity* thus tends to confirm the conception of duration as the virtual *coexistence* of all the degrees of a single and identical time.

In short, from the first page of *Duration and Simultaneity* to the last, Bergson criticizes Einstein for having confused the virtual and the actual (the introduction of the symbolic factor, that is, of a fiction, expresses this confusion). He is criticized, therefore, for having confused the two types of multiplicity, virtual and actual. At the heart of the question "Is duration one or multiple?" we find a completely different problem: Duration is a multiplicity, *but of what type?* Only the hypothesis of a single Time can, according to Bergson, account for the nature of virtual multiplicities. By confusing the two types – actual spatial multiplicity and virtual temporal multiplicity – Einstein has merely invented a new way of spatializing time. And we cannot deny the originality of his space–time and the stupendous achievement it represents for science. (Spatialization has never been pushed so far or in such a way.)[24] But this achievement is that of a symbol for expressing composites, not that of something experienced that is capable, as Proust would say, of expressing "a little time in the pure state." Being, or Time, is a *multiplicity*. But it is precisely not "multiple"; it is One, in conformity with *its* type of multiplicity.

*　　*　　*

When Bergson defends the uniqueness of time, he does not retract anything he has said previously about the virtual coexistence of various degrees of relaxation (*détente*) and contraction and the difference in kind between fluxes or actual rhythms. When he says that space and time never overlap nor "intertwine," when he maintains that only their distinction is real,[25] he does not retract any of the ambiguity of *Matter and Memory*, which consisted in integrating something of space into duration, in order to find in duration a sufficient reason (*raison suffisante*) of extension. What he condemns from the start is the whole *combination* of space and time into a badly analyzed composite, where space is considered as ready made, and time, in consequence, as a fourth dimension of space.[26] And this spatialization of time is undoubtedly inseparable from science. But Relativity is characterized by its having pushed this spatialization forward, welding the composite together in a completely new way: For, in prerelativist science, time assimilated to a fourth dimension of space is nevertheless an independent and really distinct variable. In Relativity, on the other hand, the assimilation of space to time is necessary in order to express the invariance of distance, so that it is explicitly introduced into the calculations and does not allow any real distinction to subsist. In short, Relativity has formed an especially close-knit mixture, but a mixture that is part of the Bergsonian critique of the "composite" in general.

On the other hand, from Bergson's point of view we can (in fact we must) conceive of combinations that depend on a completely different principle. Let us consider the degrees of expansion (*détente*) and of contraction, all of which coexist with one another: At the limit of expansion (*détente*), we have matter.[27] While undoubtedly, matter is not yet space, it is already extensity. A duration that is infinitely slackened and relaxed places its moments outside one another; one must have disappeared when the other appears. What these moments lose in reciprocal penetration they gain in respective spreading. What they lose in tension they gain in extension. So that, at each moment, everything tends to be spread out into an instantaneous, indefinitely divisible *continuum*, which will not prolong itself into the next instant, but will pass away, only to be reborn in the following instant, in a flicker or shiver that constantly begins again.[28] It would be sufficient to push this movement of expansion (*détente*) to its limit in order to obtain space (but space would then be found at the end of the line of differentiation as the extreme ending that is *no longer* combined with duration). Space, in effect, is not matter or extension, but the "schema" of matter, that is, the representation of the limit where the movement of expansion (*détente*) would come to an end as the external envelope of all possible extensions. In this sense, it is not matter, it is not extensity, that is in space, but the very opposite.[29] And if we think that matter has a thousand ways of becoming expanded (*détendu*) or extended, we must also say that there are all kinds of distinct extensities, all related, but still qualified, and which will finish by intermingling only in our own schema of space.

The essential point is to see how expansion (*détente*) and contraction are relative, and relative to one another. What is expanded (*détendu*) if not the contracted — and what is contracted if not the extended, the expanded (*détente*)? *This is why there is always extensity in our duration, and always duration in matter.* When we perceive, we contract millions of vibrations or elementary shocks into a felt quality; but what we contract, what we "tense" in this way, is matter, extension. In this sense there is no point in wondering if there are spatial sensations, which ones are or are not: All our sensations are extensive, all are "voluminous" and extended, although to varying degrees and in different styles, depending on the type of contraction that they carry out. And qualities belong to matter as much as to ourselves: They belong to matter, they are in matter, by virtue

87

of the vibrations and numbers that punctuate them internally. Extensities are thus still qualified, since they are inseparable from the contractions that become expanded (*détendu*) in them; and matter is never expanded (*détendu*) enough to be pure space, to stop having this minimum of contraction through which it participates in duration, through which it is part of duration.

Conversely, duration is never contracted enough to be independent of the internal matter where it operates, and of the extension that it comes to contract. Let us return to the image of the inverted cone: Its point (our present) represents the most contracted point of our duration; but it also represents our insertion in the least contracted, that is, in an infinitely relaxed (*détendu*) matter. This is why, according to Bergson, intelligence has two correlative aspects, forming an ambiguity that is essential to it: It is acquaintance with matter, it marks our adaptation to matter, it molds itself on matter; but it only does so by means of mind or duration, by placing itself in matter in a point of tension that allows it to master matter. In intelligence, one must therefore distinguish between form and sense: It has its form in matter, it finds its form with matter, that is, in the most expanded (*détendu*), but it has and finds its sense in the most contracted, through which it dominates and utilizes matter. It might therefore be said that its form separates intelligence from its meaning, but that this meaning always remains present in it, and must be rediscovered by intuition. This is why, in the final analysis, Bergson refuses all simple genesis, which would account for intelligence on the basis of an already presupposed order of matter, or which would account for the phenomena of matter on the basis of the supposed categories of intelligence. There can only be a simultaneous genesis of matter and intelligence. One step for one, one step for the other: Intelligence is contracted in matter at the same time as matter is expanded (*détendu*) in duration; both find the form that is common to them, their equilibrium, in extensity, even if intelligence in its turn pushes this form to a degree of expansion (*détente*) that matter and extensity would never have attained by themselves – that of a pure space.[30]

CHAPTER V

Élan Vital as Movement of

Differentiation

Our problem is now this: By moving from dualism to monism, from the idea of differences in kind to that of levels of expansion (*détente*) and contraction, is Bergson not reintroducing into his philosophy everything that he had condemned — the differences in degree and intensity that he so strongly criticized in *Time and Free Will*?[1] Bergson says in turn that the past and the present differ in kind and that the present is only the most contracted level or degree of the past: How can these two propositions be reconciled? The problem is no longer that of monism; we have seen how the coexisting degrees of expansion (*détente*) and contraction effectively implied a single time in which even the "fluxes" were simultaneous. The problem is that of the harmony between the dualism of differences in kind and the monism of degrees of expansion (*détente*), between the two moments of the method or the two "beyonds" the turn in experience — recognizing that the moment of dualism has not been suppressed at all, but completely retains its sense.

The critique of intensity in *Time and Free Will* is highly ambiguous. Is it directed against the very notion of intensive quantity, or merely against the idea of an intensity of psychic states? If it is true that intensity is never given in a pure experience, is it not then intensity that *gives* all the qualities with which we make experience? Hence, *Matter and Memory* recognizes intensities, degrees or vibrations in the qualities that we live as such outside ourselves and that, as such, belong to matter. There are numbers enclosed in qualities, intensities included in duration. Here again, must we speak of a contradiction in Bergson? Or are there, rather, different moments of the method, with the emphasis sometimes on one, sometimes on another, but all coexisting in a dimension of depth?

(1) Bergson begins by criticizing any vision of the world based on differences in degree or intensity. These in fact lose sight of the essential point; that is, the articulations of the real or the qualitative differences, the differences in kind. There is a difference in kind between space and duration, matter and memory, present and past, etc. We only discover this difference by dint of decomposing the composites given in experience and going beyond the "turn." We discover the differences in kind between two actual tendencies, between two actual directions toward the pure state into which each composite divides. This is the moment of pure dualism, or of the division of composites.

(2) But we can already see that it is not enough to say that the difference in kind is *between* two tendencies, between two directions, between space and duration.... For one of these two directions takes all the differences in kind on itself and all the differences in degree fall away into the other direction, the other tendency. It is duration that includes all the qualitative differences, to the point where it is defined as alteration in relation to itself. It is space that only presents differences in degree, to the point where it appears as the schema of an indef-

inite divisibility. Similarly, Memory is essentially difference and matter essentially repetition. There is therefore no longer any difference in kind between two tendencies, but a difference *between* the differences in kind that correspond to one tendency and the differences in degree that refer back to the other tendency. This is the moment of neutralized, balanced dualism.

(3) Duration, memory or spirit is difference in kind in itself and for itself; and space or matter is difference in degree outside itself and for us. Therefore, between the two there are all the *degrees of difference* or, in other words, the whole *nature of difference*. Duration is only the most contracted degree of matter, matter the most expanded (*détendu*) degree of duration. But duration is like a naturing nature (*nature naturante*), and matter a natured nature (*nature naturée*). Differences in degree are the lowest degree of Difference; differences in kind (*nature*) are the highest nature of Difference. There is no longer any dualism between nature and degrees. All the degrees coexist in a single Nature that is expressed, on the one hand, in differences in kind, and on the other, in differences in degree. This is the moment of monism: All the degrees coexist in a single Time, which is nature in itself.[2] There is no contradiction between this monism and dualism, as moments of the method. For the duality was valid between actual tendencies, between actual directions leading beyond the first turn in experience. But the unity occurs at a second turn: The coexistence of all the degrees, of all the levels is virtual, only virtual. The point of unification is itself virtual. This point is not without similarity to the One-Whole of the Platonists. All the levels of expansion (*détente*) and contraction coexist in a single Time and form a totality; but this Whole, this One, are pure virtuality. This Whole has parts, this One has a number — but only potentially.[3]

This is why Bergson is not contradicting himself when he speaks of different intensities or degrees in a virtual coexistence, in a single Time, in a simple Totality.

* * *

A philosophy like this assumes that the notion of the virtual stops being vague and indeterminate. In itself, it needs to have the highest degree of precision. This condition is only fulfilled if, starting from monism, we are able to rediscover dualism and account for it on a new plane. A fourth moment must be added to the three preceding ones — that of dualism recovered, mastered and in a sense, generated.

What does Bergson mean when he talks about *élan vital*? It is always a case of a virtuality in the process of being actualized, a simplicity in the process of differentiating, a totality in the process of dividing up: Proceeding "by dissociation and division," by "dichotomy," is the essence of life.[4] In the most familiar examples, life is divided into plant and animal; the animal is divided into instinct and intelligence; an instinct in turn divides into several directions that are actualized in different species; intelligence itself has its particular modes or actualizations. It is as if Life were merged into the very movement of differentiation, in ramified series. Movement is undoubtedly explained by the insertion of duration into matter: Duration is differentiated according to the obstacles it meets in matter, according to the materiality through which it passes, according to the kind of extension that it contracts. But differentiation does not merely have an external cause. Duration is differentiated within itself through an internal explosive force; it is only affirmed and prolonged, it only advances, in branching or ramified series.[5] Duration, to be precise, is called life when

94

it appears in this movement. Why is differentiation an "actual-ization"? Because it presupposes a unity, a virtual primordial totality that is dissociated according to the lines of differen-tiation, but that still shows its subsisting unity and totality in each line. Thus, when life is divided into plant and animal, when the animal is divided into instinct and intelligence, each side of the division, each ramification, carries the whole with it. From a certain perspective it is like an accompanying nebu-losity, testifying to its undivided origin. And there is a halo of instinct in intelligence, a nebula of intelligence in instinct, a hint of the animate in plants, and of the vegetable in animals.[6] Differentiation is always the actualization of a virtuality that persists across its actual divergent lines.

We then encounter a problem that is peculiar to Bergsonism: There are two types of division that must not be confused. According to the first type, we begin with a composite, for example the space–time mixture or the perception-image and recollection-image mixture. We divide this composite into two actual divergent lines that are different in kind and that we extend beyond the turn in experience (pure matter and pure duration, or else pure present and pure past). But now we are speaking of a completely different type of division: Our starting point is a unity, a simplicity, a virtual totality. This unity is actualized according to divergent lines differing in kind; it "explains," it develops what it had kept enclosed in a virtual manner. For example, at each instant pure duration divides in two directions, one of which is the past, the other the present; or else the *élan vital* at every instant separates into two movements, one of relaxation (*détente*) that descends into matter, the other of tension that ascends into duration. It can be seen that the divergent lines produced in the two types of division coincide and are superimposed, or at least correspond closely to each other. In the second type of division we rediscover differences in kind identical or analogous to those that had been determined in the first type. In both cases a vision of the world is criticized for only taking account of differences in degree where, more profoundly, there are differences in kind.[7] In both cases a dualism is established between tendencies that differ in kind. But this is *not* the same state of dualism, and *not* the same division. In the first type, it is a reflexive dualism, which *results from the decomposition of an impure composite*: It constitutes the first moment of the method. In the second type it is a genetic dualism, *the result of the differentiation of a Simple or a Pure*: It forms the final moment of the method that ultimately rediscovers the starting point on this new plane.

One question becomes pressing: What is the nature of this one and simple Virtual? How is it that, as early as *Time and Free Will*, then in *Matter and Memory*, Bergson's philosophy should have attributed such importance to the idea of virtuality at the very moment when it was challenging the category of possibility? It is because the "virtual" can be distinguished from the "possible" from at least two points of view. From a certain point of view, in fact, the possible is the opposite of the real, it is opposed to the real; but, in quite a different opposition, the virtual is opposed to the actual. We must take this terminology seriously: The possible has no reality (although it may have an actuality); conversely, the virtual is not actual, but *as such possesses a reality*. Here again Proust's formula best defines the states of virtuality: "real without being actual, ideal without being abstract." On the other hand, or from another point of view, the possible is that which is "realized" (or is not realized). Now the process of realization is subject to two essential rules, one of resemblance and another of limitation. For the real is supposed to be in the image of the possible that it realizes. (It simply has existence or reality added to it, which is translated by saying that, from the point of view of the concept, there is no difference between the possible and the real.) And, every possible is not realized, realization involves a limitation by which some possibles are supposed to be repulsed or thwarted, while others "pass" into the real. The virtual, on the other hand, does not have to be realized, but rather actualized; and the rules of actualization are not those of resemblance and limitation, but those of difference or divergence and of creation. When certain biologists invoke a notion of organic virtuality or potentiality and nonetheless maintain that this potentiality is actualized by simple limitation of its global capacity, they clearly fall into a confusion of the virtual and the possible.[8] For, in order to be actualized, the virtual cannot proceed by elimination or limitation, but must *create* its own lines of actualization in positive acts. The reason for this is simple: While the real is in the image and likeness of the possible that it realizes, the actual, on the other hand does *not* resemble the virtuality that it embodies. It is difference that is primary in the process of actualization — the difference between the virtual from which we begin and the actuals at which we arrive, and also the difference between the complementary lines according to which actualization takes place. In short, the characteristic of virtuality is to exist in such a way that it is actualized by being differentiated and is forced to differentiate itself, to create its lines of differentiation in order to be actualized.

Why does Bergson challenge the notion of the possible in

favor of that of the virtual? It is precisely because — by virtue of these preceding characteristics — the possible is a false notion, the source of false problems. The real is supposed to resemble it. That is to say, we give ourselves a real that is ready-made, preformed, pre-existent to itself, and that will pass into existence according to an order of successive limitations. Everything is already *completely given*: all of the real in the image, in the pseudo-actuality of the possible. Then the sleight of hand becomes obvious: If the real is said to resemble the possible, is this not in fact because the real was expected to come about by its own means, to "project backward" a ficti-tious image of it, and to claim that it was possible at any time, before it happened? In fact, it is not the real that resembles the possible, it is the possible that resembles the real, because it has been abstracted from the real once made, arbitrarily extracted from the real like a sterile double.[9] Hence, we no longer understand anything either of the mechanism of differ-ence or of the mechanism of creation.

Evolution takes place from the virtual to actuals. Evolution is actualization, actualization is creation. When we speak of biological or living evolution we must therefore avoid two mis-conceptions: that of interpreting it in terms of the "possible" that is realized, or else interpreting it in terms of pure actu-als. The first misconception obviously appears in preformism. And, contrary to preformism, evolutionism will always have the merit of reminding us that life is production, creation of differences. The whole problem is that of the nature and the causes of these differences. The vital differences or variations can certainly be conceived of as purely accidental. But three objections to an interpretation of this kind arise:

(1) since they are due to chance, these variations, how-

ever small they are, would remain external, "indifferent" to
each other;

(2) since they are external, they could not logically enter
into anything but relations of association and addition with
one another;

(3) since they are indifferent, they could not even have the
means to really enter into such relations (for there would be
no reason why the small successive variations should link up
and add together in the same direction; nor any reason for
sudden and simultaneous variations to be coordinated into a
livable whole).[10]

If we invoke the action of the environment and the influ-
ence of external conditions, the three objections persist in
another form: For the differences are still interpreted from the
perspective of a purely external causality. In their nature they
would only be passive effects, elements that could be abstractly
combined or added together. In their relationships they would,
however, be incapable of functioning "as a bloc," so as to con-
trol or utilize their causes.[11]

The mistake of evolutionism is, thus, to conceive of vital
variations as so many actual determinations that should then
combine on a single line. The three requirements of a philosophy of life are as follows:

(1) the vital difference can only be experienced and thought
of as internal difference; it is only in this sense that the "tendency to change" is not accidental, and that the variations
themselves find an internal cause in that tendency;

(2) these variations do not enter into relationships of association and addition, but on the contrary, they enter into relationships of dissociation or division;

(3) they therefore involve a virtuality that is actualized

99

according to the lines of divergence; so that evolution does not move from one actual term to another actual term in a homogeneous unilinear series, but from a virtual term to the heterogeneous terms that actualize it along a ramified series.[12]

But this leads to the question of how the Simple or the One, "the original identity," has the power to be differentiated. The answer is already contained in *Matter and Memory*. And the linkage between *Creative Evolution* and *Matter and Memory* is perfectly rigorous. We know that the *virtual as virtual has a reality*; this reality, extended to the whole universe, consists in all the coexisting degrees of expansion (*détente*) and contraction. A gigantic memory, a universal cone in which everything coexists with itself, except for the differences of level. On each of these levels there are some "outstanding points," which are like remarkable points peculiar to it. All these levels or degrees and all these points are themselves virtual. They belong to a single Time; they coexist in a Unity; they are enclosed in a Simplicity; they form the potential parts of a Whole that is itself virtual. They are *the reality of this virtual*. This was the sense of the theory of virtual multiplicities that inspired Bergsonism from the start. When the virtuality is actualized, is differentiated, is "developed," when it actualizes and develops its parts, it does so according to lines that are divergent, but each of which corresponds to a particular degree in the virtual totality. There is here no longer any coexisting whole; there are merely lines of actualization, *some successive, others simultaneous*, but each representing an actualization of the whole in one direction and not combining with other lines or other directions. Nevertheless, each of these lines corresponds to one of these degrees that all coexist in the virtual; it actualizes its level, while separating it from the others; it embodies its prominent points, while being unaware of everything that happens on other levels.[13] We must think of it as follows: When duration is divided into matter and life, then life into plant and animal, different levels of contraction, which only coexist insofar as they remain virtual, are actualized. And when the animal instinct is itself divided into various instincts, or when a particular instinct is itself divided according to species, levels are again separated, or are actually cut out in the region of the animal or of the genus. And however strictly the lines of actualization correspond to the levels or the virtual degrees of expansion (*détente*) or contraction, it should not be thought that the lines of actualization confine themselves to tracing these levels or degrees, to reproducing them by simple resemblance. For what coexisted in the virtual ceases to coexist in the actual and is distributed in lines or parts that cannot be summed up, each one retaining the whole, except from a certain perspective, from a certain point of view. These lines of differentiation are therefore truly creative: They only actualize by inventing, they create in these conditions the physical, vital or psychical representative of the ontological level that they embody.

If we concentrate only on the actuals that conclude each line, we establish relationships between them — whether of gradation or opposition. Between plant and animal, for example, between animal and man, we now only see differences in degree. Or we will situate a fundamental opposition in each one of them: We will see in one the negative of the other, the inversion of the other, or the obstacle that is opposed to the other. Bergson often expresses himself in this way, in terms of contrariety: Matter is presented as the obstacle that the *élan vital* must get around, and materiality, as the inversion of the

Summary Diagram of Differentiation (CE, Ch. 2)

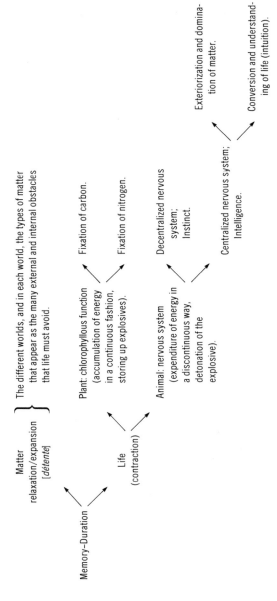

Memory–Duration

Matter
relaxation/expansion
[*détente*]

Life
(contraction)

The different worlds, and in each world, the types of matter
that appear as the many external and internal obstacles
that life must avoid.

Plant: chlorophyllous function
(accumulation of energy
in a continuous fashion,
storing up explosives).

Fixation of carbon.

Fixation of nitrogen.

Animal: nervous system
(expenditure of energy in
a discontinuous way,
detonation of the
explosive).

Decentralized nervous
system;
Instinct.

Centralized nervous system;
Intelligence.

Exteriorization and domination of matter.

Conversion and understanding of life (intuition).

movement of life.[14] It should not, however, be thought that Bergson is going back to a conception of the negative that he had previously condemned, any more than he returns to a theory of deteriorations. For one only has to replace the actual terms in the movement that produces them to bring them back to the virtuality actualized in them, in order to see that differentiation is never a negation but a creation, and that difference is never negative but essentially positive and creative.

*   *   *

We always rediscover the laws common to these lines of actualization or of differentiation. There is a correlation between life and matter, between expansion *(détente)* and contraction, which shows the coexistence of their respective degrees in the virtual Whole, and their essential relativity in the process of actualization. Each line of life is related to a type of matter that is not merely an external environment, but in terms of which the living being manufactures a body, a form, for itself. This is why the living being, in relation to matter, appears primarily as the stating of a problem, and the capacity to solve problems: The construction of an eye, for example, is primarily the solution to a problem posed in terms of light.[15] And each time, we will say that the solution was as good as it could have been, given the way in which the problem was stated, and the means that the living being had at its disposal to solve it. (It is in this way that, if we compare a similar instinct in various species, we ought not to say that it is more or less complete, more or less perfected, but that it is as perfect as it can be in varying degrees.)[16] It is nevertheless clear that each vital solution is not in itself a success: By dividing the animal in two, Arthropods and Vertebrates, we have not taken into account

103

the two other directions, Echinoderms and Mollusks, which are a setback for the *élan vital*.[17] Everything takes place as though living beings themselves also stated false problems for themselves in which they risk losing their way. Moreover, if every solution is a relative success in relation to the conditions of the problem or the environment, it is still a relative setback, in relation to the movement that invents it: Life as *movement* alienates itself in the material *form* that it creates; by actualizing itself, by differentiating itself, it loses "contact with the rest of itself." Every species is thus an arrest of movement; it could be said that the living being turns on itself and *closes itself*.[18] It cannot be otherwise, since the Whole is only virtual, dividing itself by being acted out. It cannot assemble its actual parts that remain external to each other: The Whole is never "given." And, in the actual, an irreducible pluralism reigns — as many worlds as living beings, all "closed" on themselves.

But we must, in another oscillation, be delighted that the *Whole* is not given. This is the constant theme of Bergsonism from the outset: The confusion of space and time, the assimilation of time into space, make us think that the whole is given, even if only in principle, even if only in the eyes of God. And this is the mistake that is common to mechanism and to finalism. The former assumes that everything is calculable in terms of a state; the latter, that everything is determinable in terms of a program: In any event, time is only there now as a screen that hides the eternal from us, or that shows us successively what a God or a superhuman intelligence would see in a single glance.[19] Now this illusion is inevitable as soon as we spatialize time. Indeed, in space it is sufficient to have a dimension supplementary to those where a phenomenon happens for the movement in the course of happening to appear to us as a ready-made form. If we consider time as a fourth dimension of space, this fourth dimension will thus be assumed to contain all the possible forms of the universe as a whole; and movement in space, as well as flowing in time, will now only be appearances linked to the three dimensions.[20] But the fact that real space has only three dimensions, that Time is not a dimension of space, really means this: There is an efficacity, a positivity of time, that is identical to a "hesitation" of things and, in this way, to creation in the world.[21]

It is clear that there is a Whole of duration. But this whole is virtual. It is actualized according to divergent lines; but these lines *do not* form a whole on their own account, and do not resemble what they actualize. If the choice is between mechanism and finalism, finalism is preferable; *providing that it is corrected in two ways.* On the one hand, it is right to compare the living being to the whole of the universe, but it is wrong to interpret this comparison as if it expressed a kind of analogy between two closed totalities (macrocosm and microcosm). The finality of the living being exists only insofar as it is essentially open onto a totality that is itself open: "finality is external, or it is nothing at all."[22] It is thus the whole classical comparison that takes on another meaning; it is not the whole that closes like an organism, it is the organism that opens onto a whole, like this virtual whole.

On the other hand, there is a proof of finality to the extent that we discover similar actualizations, identical structures or apparatuses on divergent lines (for example, the eye in the Mollusk and in the Vertebrate). The example will be all the more significant the further apart the lines are, and the more the organ that is similar is obtained by dissimilar means.[23] We see here how, in the process of actualization, the very category of resemblance finds itself subordinated to that of divergence, difference or differentiation. While actual forms or products can resemble each other, the movements of production do not resemble each other, nor do the products resemble the virtuality that they embody. This is why actualization, differentiation, are a genuine creation. The Whole must *create* the divergent lines according to which it is actualized and the dissimilar means that it utilizes on each line. There is finality because life does not operate without directions; but there is no "goal," because these directions do not pre-exist ready-made, and are themselves created "along with" the act that runs through them.[24] Each line of actualization corresponds to a virtual level; but each time, it must invent the figure of this correspondence and create the means for the development of that which was only enveloped in order to distinguish that which was confused.

*   *   *

Duration, Life, is *in principle* (*en droit*) memory, in principle consciousness, in principle freedom. "In principle" means virtually. The whole question (*quid facti?*) is knowing under what conditions duration becomes *in fact* consciousness of self, how life *actually* accedes to a memory and freedom of fact.[25] Bergson's answer is that it is only on the line of Man that the *élan vital* successfully "gets through"; man in this sense *is* "the purpose of the entire process of evolution."[26] It could be said that in man, and only in man, the actual becomes adequate to the virtual. It could be said that man is capable of rediscovering all the levels, all the degrees of expansion (*détente*) and contraction that coexist in the virtual Whole. As if he were capable of all the frenzies and brought about in himself successively everything that, elsewhere, can only be embodied in different species. Even in his dreams he rediscovers or prepares matter. And durations that are inferior or superior to him are still internal to him. Man therefore creates a differentiation that is valid for the Whole, and he alone traces out an open direction that is able to express a whole that is itself open. Whereas the other directions are closed and go round in circles, whereas a distinct "plane" of nature corresponds to each one, man is capable of scrambling the planes, of going beyond his own plane as his own condition, in order finally to express naturing Nature.[27]

How does this privilege of man come about? At first sight, its origin is a humble one. Every contraction of duration still being relative to an expansion (*détente*), and every life to a matter, the point of departure is in a certain state of cerebral matter. We recall that this latter "analyzed" the received excitation, selected the reaction, made possible an *interval* between excitation and reaction; nothing here goes beyond the physico-chemical properties of a particularly complicated type of matter. But, as we have seen, it is the whole of memory that descends into this interval, and that becomes actual. It is the whole of freedom that is actualized. On man's line of differentiation, the *élan vital* was able to use matter to create an instrument of freedom, "to make a machine which should triumph over mechanism," "to use the determinism of nature to pass through the meshes of the net which this very determinism had spread."[28] Freedom has precisely this physical sense: "to detonate" an explosive, to use it for more and more powerful movements.[29]

But where does this starting point seem to lead? To perception; and also to a utilitarian memory, since useful recollections are actualized in the cerebral interval; and to intelligence as the organ of domination and utilization of matter. We even understand that men form *societies*. It is not that society is solely or essentially intelligent. From the outset, human societies undoubtedly imply a certain intelligent comprehension of needs and a certain rational organization of activities. But they are also formed, and only subsist through irrational or even absurd factors. Take, for example, obligation: It has no rational ground. Each particular obligation is conventional and can border on the absurd; the only thing that is grounded is the obligation to have obligations, "the whole of obligation"; and it is not grounded in reason, but in a requirement of nature, in a kind of "virtual instinct," that is, on a counterpart that nature produces *in* the reasonable being in order to compensate for the partiality of his intelligence. Each line of differentiation, being exclusive, seeks to recapture, by its own means, the advantages of the other line. Thus, in their separation, instinct and intelligence are such that the one produces an ersatz of intelligence, the other, an equivalent of instinct. This is the "story-telling function": virtual instinct, creator of gods, inventor of religions, that is, of fictitious representations "which will stand up to the representation of the real and which will succeed, by the intermediary of intelligence itself, in thwarting intellectual work." And as in the case of obligation, each god is contingent, or even absurd, but what is natural, necessary and grounded is *having* gods; it is the pantheon of gods.[30] In short, sociability (in the human sense) can only exist *in* intelligent beings, but it is not grounded *on* their intelligence: Social life is immanent to intelligence, it begins with it but does not derive from it. Hence our problem appears to have become more complicated instead of being solved. For if we consider intelligence and sociability, both in their complementarity and in their difference, nothing yet justifies man's privilege. The societies that he forms are no less closed than animal species; they form part of a plan (*plan*) of nature, as much as animal species and societies; and man goes round in circles in his society just as much as the species do in theirs or ants in their domain.[31] Nothing here seems to be capable of giving man the previously mentioned exceptional opening, as the power of going beyond his "plane" (*plan*) and his condition.

Unless this kind of play of intelligence and of society, this small interval between the two, is itself a decisive factor. The small intracerebral interval has already made intelligence possible, and the actualization of a memory useful. Moreover, thanks to it, the body imitates the whole life of the mind, and we were able with a leap to place ourselves in the pure past. We now find ourselves before *another intercerebral interval* between intelligence itself and society: Is it not this "hesitation" of the intelligence that will be able to imitate the superior "hesitation" of things in duration, and that will allow man, with a leap, to break the circle of closed societies? At first sight, the answer is no. For, if intelligence hesitates and sometimes rebels, it is primarily in the name of an egoism that it seeks to preserve against social requirements.[32] And while society makes itself obeyed it is thanks to the story-telling function, which persuades the intelligence that it is in its interest to confirm the social obligation. We therefore seem to be constantly sent back from one term to another. But everything changes when something appears in the interval.

What is it that appears in the interval between intelligence and society (in the same way as the recollection-image appeared in the cerebral interval appropriate to intelligence)? We cannot reply: It is intuition. In fact, we must on the contrary carry out a genesis of intuition, that is, determine the way in which intelligence itself was converted or is converted into intuition. And if we recall, according to the laws of differentiation, that intelligence, in separating itself from instinct, nevertheless keeps an equivalent of instinct that would be like the nucleus of intuition. We are not saying anything of importance, for this equivalent of instinct finds itself completely mobilized in the closed society as such, through the story-telling function.[33] Bergson's real answer is completely different: What appears in the interval is *emotion*. In this answer, "We have no choice."[34] Only emotion differs in nature from both intelligence and instinct, from both intelligent individual egoism and quasi-instinctive social pressure. Obviously no one denies that egoism produces emotions; and even more so social pressure, with all the fantasies of the story-telling function. But in both these cases, emotion is always connected to a representation on which it is supposed to depend. We are then placed in a composite of emotion and of representation, without noticing that it is potential (*en puissance*), the nature of emotion as pure element. The latter in fact precedes all representation, itself generating new ideas. It does not have, strictly speaking, an object, but merely an *essence* that spreads itself over various objects, animals, plants and the whole of nature. "Imagine a piece of music which expresses love. It is not love for a particular person.... The quality of love will depend upon its essence and not upon its object."[35] Although personal, it is not individual; transcendent, it is like the God in us. "When music cries, it is humanity, it is the whole of nature which cries with it. Truly speaking, it does not introduce these feelings in us; it introduces us rather into them, like the passers-by that might be nudged in a dance." In short, emotion is creative (first, because it expresses the whole of creation, then because *it* creates the work in which it is expressed; and finally, because it communicates a little of this creativity to spectators or hearers).

The little interval "between the pressure of society and the resistance of intelligence" defines a variability appropriate to human societies. Now, by means of this interval, something extraordinary is produced or embodied: creative emotion. This no longer has anything to do with the pressures of society, nor with the disputes of the individual. It no longer has anything to do with an individual who contests or even invents, nor with a society that constrains, that persuades or even tells stories.[36] It has only made use of their circular play in order to break the circle, just as Memory uses the circular play of excitation and reaction to embody recollections in images. And what is this creative emotion, if not precisely a cosmic Memory, that actualizes all the levels at the same time, that liberates man from the plane (*plan*) or the level that is proper to him, in order to make him a creator, adequate to the whole movement of creation?[37] This liberation, this embodiment of cosmic memory in creative emotions, undoubtedly only takes place in privileged souls. It leaps from one soul to another, "every now and then," crossing closed deserts. But to each member of a closed society, if he opens himself to it, it communicates a kind of reminiscence, an excitement that allows him to follow. And from soul to soul, it traces the design of an *open* society, a society of creators, where we pass from one genius to another, through the intermediary of disciples or spectators or hearers.

It is the genesis of intuition in intelligence. If man accedes to the open creative totality, it is therefore by acting, by creating rather than by contemplating. In philosophy itself, there is still too much alleged contemplation: Everything happens as if intelligence were already imbued with emotion, thus with intuition, but not sufficiently so for creating in conformity to this emotion.[38] Thus the great souls — to a greater extent than philosophers — are those of artists and mystics (at least those of a Christian mysticism that Bergson describes as being completely superabundant activity, action, creation).[39] At the limit, it is the mystic who plays with the whole of creation, who invents an expression of it whose adequacy increases with its dynamism. Servant of an open and finite God (such are the characteristics of the *Élan Vital*), the mystical soul actively plays the whole of the universe, and reproduces the opening of a Whole in which there is nothing to see or to contemplate. Already motivated by emotion, the philosopher extracted the lines that divided up the composites given in experience. He prolonged the outline to beyond the "turn"; he showed in the distance the virtual point at which they all met. Everything happens as if that which remained indeterminate in philosophical intuition gained a new kind of determination in mystical intuition — as though the properly philosophical "probability" extended itself into mystical certainty. Undoubtedly philosophy can only consider the mystical soul from the outside and from the point of view of its lines of probability.[40] But it is precisely the existence of mysticism that gives a higher probability to this final transmutation into certainty, and also gives, as it were, an envelope or a limit to all the aspects of method.

★   ★   ★

At the outset we asked: What is the relationship between the three fundamental concepts of Duration, Memory and the *Élan Vital*? What progress do they indicate in Bergson's philosophy? It seems to us that Duration essentially defines a virtual multiplicity (*what differs in nature*). Memory then appears as the coexistence of all the *degrees of difference* in this multiplicity, in this virtuality. The *élan vital*, finally, designates the actualization of this virtual according to the *lines of differentiation* that correspond to the degrees — up to this precise line of man where the *Élan Vital* gains self-consciousness.

A Return to Bergson

A "return to Bergson" does not only mean a renewed admiration for a great philosopher but a renewal or an extension of his project today, in relation to the transformations of life and society, in parallel with the transformations of science. Bergson himself considered that he had made metaphysics a rigorous discipline, one capable of being continued along new paths which constantly appear in the world. It seems to us that the return to Bergson, understood in this way, rests on three main features.

Intuition

Bergson saw intuition not as an appeal to the ineffable, a participation in a feeling or a lived identification, but as a true method. This method sets out, firstly, to determine the conditions of problems, that is to say, to expose false problems or wrongly posed questions, and to discover the variables under which a given problem must be stated as such. The means used by intuition are, on the one hand, a cutting up or division of reality in a given domain, according to lines of different natures and, on the other hand, an intersection of lines which are taken from various domains and which converge. It is this complex linear operation, consisting in a cutting up according to articulations and an intersecting according to convergences, which leads to the proper posing of a problem, in such a way that the solution itself depends on it.

Science and Metaphysics

Bergson did not merely criticize science as if it went no further than space, the solid, the immobile. Rather, he thought that the Absolute has two "halves," to which science and metaphysics correspond. Thought divides into two paths in a single impetus, one toward matter, its bodies and movements, and the other toward spirit, its qualities and changes. Thus, from antiquity, just as physics related movement to privileged positions and moments, metaphysics constituted transcendent eternal forms from which these positions derive. But "modern" science begins, on the contrary, when movement is related to "any instant whatever": it demands a new metaphysics which now only takes into account immanent and constantly varying durations. For Bergson, duration becomes the metaphysical correlate of modern science. He, of course, wrote a book, *Duration and Simultaneity,* in which he considered Einstein's Relativity. This book led to so much misunderstanding because it was thought that Bergson was seeking to refute or correct Einstein, while in fact he wanted, by means of the new feature of duration, to give the theory of Relativity the metaphysics it lacked. And in this masterpiece, *Matter and Memory,* Bergson draws, from a scientific conception of the brain to which he himself made important contributions, the requirements of a new metaphysic of memory. For Bergson, science is never "reductionist" but, on the contrary, demands a metaphysics — without which it would remain abstract, deprived of meaning or intuition. To continue

Bergson's project today, means for example to constitute a meta-physical image of thought corresponding to the new lines, openings, traces, leaps, dynamisms, discovered by a molecular biology of the brain: new linkings and re-linkings in thought.

Multiplicities

From *Time and Free Will* onward, Bergson defines duration as a multiplicity, a type of multiplicity. This is a strange word, since it makes the multiple no longer an adjective but a genuine noun. Thus, he exposes the traditional theme of the one and the multiple as a false problem. The origin of the word, Multiplicity or Variety, is physico-mathematical (deriving from Riemann). It is difficult to believe that Bergson was not aware of the scientific origin of the term and the novelty of its metaphysical use. Bergson moves toward a distinction between two major types of multiplicities, the one discrete or discontinuous, the other continuous, the one spatial and the other temporal, the one actual, the other virtual. This is a fundamental theme of the encounter with Einstein. Once again, Bergson intends to give multiplicities the metaphysics which their scientific treatment demands. This is perhaps one of the least appreciated aspects of his thought – the constitution of a logic of multiplicities.

To rediscover Bergson is to follow or carry forward his approach in these three directions. It should be noted that these three themes are also to be found in phenomenology – intuition as method, philosophy as rigorous science and the new logic as theory of multiplicities. It is true that these notions are under-stood very differently in the two cases. There is nevertheless a possible convergence as can be seen in psychiatry where berg-sonism inspired the works of Minkowski (*Le temps vécu*) and in phenomenology those of Binswanger (*Le cas Susan Urban*), in his explorations of space-times in psychoses. Bergsonism makes possible a whole pathology of duration. In an outstanding article on "paramnesia" (false recognition), Bergson invokes metaphysics to show how a memory is not constituted after present perception, but is strictly contemporaneous with it, since at each instant duration divides into two simultaneous tendencies, one of which goes toward the future and the other falls back into the past. He also invokes psychology, in order to then show how a failure of adaptation can make memory invest the present as such. Scientific hypothesis and metaphysical thesis are constantly combined in Bergson in the reconstitution of complete experience.

GILLES DELEUZE
Paris, July 1988
Translated by Hugh Tomlinson

Notes

TRANSLATORS' INTRODUCTION

1. *Bergson*, Oxford: Oxford University Press, 1985, p. 2.

2. See Gilles Deleuze and Claire Parnet, *Dialogues* (translated by Hugh Tomlinson and Barbara Habberjam). London: The Athlone Press, 1987, pp. 14-15.

3. "Lettre à Michel Cressole," in Michel Cressole, *Deleuze*. Paris: Editions Universitaires, 1973, p. 111.

4. *Dialogues*, op. cit., p. 15.

5. *Ibid.*, pp. vii-viii.

6. Gillian Rose, *Dialectic of Nihilism*, Oxford: Basil Blackwell, 1984, Chapter 6.

7. Gilles Deleuze, *Cinema 1: The Movement-Image* (translated by Hugh Tomlinson and Barbara Habberjam). London: The Athlone Press, 1986, Chapters 1 and 4; and Gilles Deleuze, *Cinema 2: The Time-Image* (translated by Hugh Tomlinson and Robert Galeta). London: The Athlone Press, 1988, Chapters 3 and 5.

8. *Time and Free Will, Matter and Memory, Creative Evolution*, and *Mind-Energy*. For full references, see p. 11.

9. *Critique of Pure Reason*, A84/B116; see Gilles Deleuze, *Kant's Critical Philosophy* (translated by Hugh Tomlinson and Barbara Habberjam). London: The Athlone Press, 1984, p. 11ff.

119

Chapter I

1. CM, 33 (1271, 25).

2. *Lettre à Höffding*, 1916 (cf. *Ecrits et Paroles*, Vol. 3, p. 456).

3. On the use of the word *intuition*, and on the genesis of the notion in TF and MM the reader is referred to M. Husson's book, *L'intellectualisme de Bergson*, Presses Universitaires de France, 1947, pp. 6-10.

4. CM, 37-38 (1274-1275, 29-30).

5. CM, 58-59 (1293, 51-52). On the "semi-divine state," cf. CM, 75 (1306, 68).

6. According to Bergson, the category of *problem* has a greater *biological* importance than the negative category of *need*.

7. CM, 113 (1336, 105). The arrangement of examples varies in Bergson's texts. This is not surprising, because each false problem, as we shall see, presents the two aspects in variable proportions. On freedom and intensity as false problems, cf. CM, 28-29 (1268, 20).

8. CM, 118 (1339, 110). On the critique of disorder and of nonbeing, cf. also CE, 242-243 (683, 223ff.) and 302-303 (730, 278ff.).

9. CM, 59-60 (1293-1294, 52-53).

10. Cf. TF, Ch. 1.

11. CM, 73-74 (1304-1305, 66).

12. Cf. a very important note in CM, 303-304 (1306, 68) [same reference as note 5].

13. CE, 167 (623, 152).

14. Qualitative differences or the articulations of the real are constant terms and themes in Bergson's philosophy: cf., in particular, the Introduction to CM, *passim*. It is in this sense that one can speak of a Platonism in Bergson (cf. the method of division). He loves to quote the text of Plato on cutting up and the good cook. Cf. CE, 172 (627, 157).

15. CE, 346 (764, 318).

16. For example, intelligence and instinct form a composite which in its *pure* state can only be dissociated into tendencies, cf. CE, 150-151 (610, 137).

17. On the opposition "in fact - in principle," cf. MM, Ch. 1 - notably 73 (213, 68). And on the "presence-representation" distinction, MM, 35 (185, 32).

18. MM, 48 (197, 47).

19. MM, 36 (186, 33): "Now, if living beings are within the universe just 'centers of indetermination,' and if the degree of this indetermination is measured by the number and rank of their function, we can conceive that their mere presence is equivalent to the suppression of all those parts of objects in which their functions find no interest."

20. The line does not need to be entirely homogeneous, it can be a broken line. Thus affectivity is qualitatively distinct from perception, but not in the same way as memory: Whereas a *pure* memory is opposed to pure perception, affectivity is more like an "impurity" which troubles perception: cf. MM, 58 (207, 60). We will see later how affectivity, memory, etc., denote very diverse aspects of subjectivity.

21. MM, 67 (214, 69). Translation modified.

22. MM, 184 (321, 205).

23. MM, 185 (321, 206). Bergson often seems to criticize the infinitesimal analysis: Although it reduces ad infinitum the intervals that it considers, it is still content to recompose movement with covered space: for example, TF 119-120 (79-80, 89). But more profoundly, Bergson requires that metaphysics, for its part, carry out a revolution which is *analogous* to that of calculus in science: cf. CE, 357-372 (773-786, 329-344). And metaphysics should even draw inspiration from the "generative idea of our mathematics," in order to "carry out qualitative differentiations and integrations": CM, 216-217 (1423, 215). [see also n. 24]

24. Cf. CM, 216-217 (1416, 206). And 228 (1425, 218): "Philosophy should be an effort to go beyond the human state." (The previously quoted text, on *the turning point of experience*, is a commentary on this formula.)

25. CM, 157-159 (1370, 148-149).

26. MR, 237 (1186, 263).

27. CM, 87-88 (1315, 80).

28. MR, 252-253 (1199-1200, 280-281).

29. ME, 6-7 (817-818, 4), 35 (835, 27).

30. Cf. MM, 71 (218, 74): "Questions relating to subject and object, to their distinction and their union, should be put in terms of time rather than space."

31. CM, 38-39 (1275, 30).

32. CE, 13 (502, 10). In this context, Bergson grants sugar duration only insofar as it participates in the whole of the universe. The meaning of this restriction will become clearer in Chapter 4.

33. CM, 217 (1416-1417, 206-208).

34. CM, 65-71 (129-130, 58-64).

35. CE, 236-237 (679, 217). Translation modified.

36. MR, 202 (1156, 225). Translation modified.

37. Cf. CM, 42-43 (1278ff., 34ff.). And CM, 112 (1335, 104): Intelligence "touches one of the sides of the absolute, as our consciousness touches another."

38. CM, 68 (1300, 61).

CHAPTER II

1. See A. Robinet's excellent analysis on this point, in *Bergson*, Seghers, 1965, pp. 28ff.

2. Admittedly, as early as *Time and Free Will* Bergson points out the problem of a genesis of the concept of *space*, starting from a perception of extensity, cf. 95-97 (64-65, 71-72).

3. TF, Ch. 2 and Ch. 3, 83-84 (107, 122). The badly analyzed composite or the confusion of the two multiplicities precisely defines false notions of intensity.

4. On Riemann's theory of multiplicities cf. G.B.R. Riemann, *Oeuvres Mathématiques* (French Translation edited by Gauthier-Villars, "Sur les hypothèses qui servent de fondement à la géometrie"); and H. Weyl, *Temps, Espace, Matière*. Husserl too gained inspiration from Riemann's theory of multiplicities, although in quite a different way from Bergson.

5. TF, 83-84 (57, 62).

6. MM, 71-72 (218-219, 75-76).

7. CM, 137 (1353, 127).

8. Cf. MM, 206 (341, 231). "As long as we are dealing with space, we may carry the division as long as we please; we change in no way the nature of what is divided."

9. TF, 81-82 (55-56, 60-61).

10. TF, 84 (57, 62).

11. TF, 121 (81, 90).

12. The objective is, effectively, defined by the parts that are actually and not virtually perceived: TF, 84-85 (57, 63). This implies that the subjective, on the other hand, is defined by the virtuality of its parts. Let us return then to the text: "We apply the term subjective to what seems to be completely and adequately known, and the term objective to that which is known in such a way that a constantly increasing number of new impressions could be substituted for the idea which we actually have of it": TF 83 (57, 62). Taken literally, these definitions are strange. By virtue of the context, one might even wish to reverse them. For is it not the objective (matter) that, being without virtuality, has a being similar to its "appearing" and finds itself therefore adequately known? And is it not the subjective that can always be divided into two parts of another nature, which it only contained virtually? We might almost be inclined to think it a printing error. But the terms Bergson uses are justified from another point of view. In the case of subjective duration, the divisions are only valid insofar as they are effectuated, that is, actualized: "The parts of our duration are one with the successive moments of the act which divides it...and if our consciousness can only distinguish in a given interval a definite number of elementary acts, if it terminates the division at a given point, there also terminates the divisibility": MM, 206 (341, 232). It can therefore be said that, on each of its levels, the division adequately gives us the indivisible nature of the thing while, in the case of objective matter, the division does not even need to be effectuated: We know in

advance that it is possible without any change in the nature of the thing. In this sense, if it is true that the object contains nothing *other* than what we know, it nonetheless always contains *more*: MM, 147 (289, 164); it is therefore not adequately known.

13. CM, 206-207 (1408, 196-197).

14. The denunciation of the Hegelian dialectic as false movement, abstract movement, failure to comprehend real movement, is a frequent theme in Kierkegaard, Marx, and Nietzsche, albeit in very different contexts.

15. Cf. Plato, *Philebus.*

16. CM, 207-217 (1409-1416, 197-207). This text is close to the passage in Plato where he condemns the pliancy of the dialectic. We have seen that the Bergsonian method of division had a Platonic inspiration. The point of contact between Bergson and Plato is in fact the search for a procedure capable of determining in each case the "measure," the "what" or the "how many." It is true that Plato thought a refined dialectic could meet these requirements. Bergson, on the other hand, considers the dialectic in general, including that of Plato, to be valid only for the beginnings of philosophy (and of the history of philosophy). The dialectic passes by a true method of division, it can do nothing other than carve out the real according to articulations that are wholly formal or verbal. Cf. CM, 95 (1321, 87): "There is nothing more natural than that philosophy should at first have been content with this, and that it began by being pure dialectic. It had nothing else at its disposal. A Plato, an Aristotle, adopt the cutting out of reality that they find already made in language . . . ."

17. TF, 110 (74, 82).

18. Cf. a very important text in CE, 321ff. (757ff., 310ff.): "But all movement is articulated inwardly," etc.

19. TF, 227 (148, 170) and 209-219 (137, 157). Translation modified.

CHAPTER III

1. ME, 8 (818, 5); CM, 211 (1411, 201); MM, 34 (184, 31) The emphasis is

ours in each of these texts. These two forms of memory should not be confused with those discussed by Bergson at the beginning of Chapter 2 of MM, 78 (225, 83); this is a completely different principle of distinction, cf. note 34.

2. CM, 193 (1398, 183).

3. Cf. ME, 13-14 (820, 8).

4. Cf. MM, 58 (206, 59).

5. MM, 77 (223, 81).

6. CM, 87 (1315, 80). Translation modified.

7. MM, 148-149 (290, 165-166).

8. Nevertheless, on another occasion, Bergson maintained that there was only a difference in degree between being and being useful: In fact, perception is only distinguished from its object because it retains solely that which is useful to us (cf. MM, Ch. 1). There is *more* in the object than in perception, but there is nothing that is of a different kind. But in this case, the being is merely that of matter or of the perceived object, thus a *present being* whose only distinction from the *useful* is one of degree.

9. CM, 88-89 (1316, 81).

10. Jean Hyppolite gives us a profound analysis of this aspect. He attacks "psychologistic" interpretations of *Matter & Memory*: Cf. "Du bergsonisme à l'existentialisme," *Mercure de France*, July, 1949; and "Aspects divers de la mémoire chez Bergson," *Revue internationale de philosophie*, October, 1949.

11. MM, 133-134 (276-277, 148).

12. The expression "at once" (*d'emblée*) is frequently used in Chapters 2 and 3 of MM.

13. Cf. MM, 116 (261, 129): "the hearer places himself at once in the midst of the corresponding ideas...."

14. MM, 135 (278, 150). Translation modified.

15. Cf. ME, 157-160 (913-914, 130-131): "I hold that the *formation of recollection is never posterior to the formation of perception; it is contemporaneous with it....* For suppose recollection is not created at the same moment as perception: At what moment will it begin to exist? ... The more we reflect, the

more impossible it is to imagine any way in which the recollection can arise if it is not created step by step with the perception itself...."

16. A comparison could also be made here between Bergson and Proust. Their conception of time is extremely different, but both acknowledge a kind of pure past, a being in itself of the past. According to Proust this being in itself can be lived, experienced by virtue of a coincidence between two instants of time. But according to Bergson, pure recollection or pure past are not a domain of the lived, even in *paramnesia*; we only experience a recollection-image.

17. The metaphor of the cone is first introduced in MM, 152 (293, 169).

18. MM, 241-242 (371, 272).

19. On this *metaphysical repetition* cf. MM, 103-104 (250, 115); 161-162 (302, 181).

20. Cf. MM, 103-104 (249-250, 114). Bergson shows clearly how we necessarily believe that the past *follows* the present as soon as we establish only a *difference in degree* between the two; cf. ME, 160-161 (914, 132): "The perception being defined as a strong state and the recollection as a weak state, the recollection of a perception being necessarily then nothing else than the same perception weakened, it seems to us that memory ought to have to wait in order to register a perception in the unconscious. Indeed, it must wait until the whole of it goes to sleep. And so we suppose the recollection of a perception cannot be created while the perception is being created nor can it be developed at the same time." Translation modified.

21. MM, 170 (309-310, 190).

22. MM, 134 (277, 148).

23. MM, 130 (274-275, 145).

24. MM, 168-169 (307-308, 188) (our emphasis).

25. For example, in the passage that we have just quoted.

26. In fact, the level must be actualized no less than the recollection that it bears. Cf. MM, 242 (371, 272): "These planes, moreover, are not given as ready-made things superposed the one on the other. Rather they exist virtu-

ally, with that existence which is proper to things of the spirit. The intellect, forever moving in the interval which separates them, unceasingly finds them again or creates them anew...."

27. MM, 168 (308, 188): "without dividing...."

28. ME, 195-198 (936-938, 161-163). Hence the metaphor of the pyramid to represent the dynamic schema: "We will descend again from the summit of the pyramid toward the base...." It is clear that the pyramid is very different from the cone and denotes a completely different movement, with a different orientation. However, in another text (ME, 116 [886, 95]), Bergson evokes the pyramid as the synonym of the cone; the explanation for this is in the ambiguity pointed out above, note 25.

29. MM, 104 (249-250, 114-115).

30. On these two extremes, cf. MM, 153 (294, 170).

31. MM, 120 (265, 133). Translation modified. And MM, 99 (245, 108): "the last phase of the realization of a recollection - the phase of action...." Translation modified.

32. Cf. MM, 92-93 (238-240, 100-102); 98 (243-244, 107); 112 (255-256, 121-122). Above all the *motor scheme* should not be confused with the *dynamic schema*. Both intervene in actualization but at completely different phases: The former is purely sensory-motor, the latter psychological and mnemonic.

33. MM, 97 (241, 104).

34. Cf. MM, 108-109 (252-253, 118-119).

35. MM, 98 (244, 107). There are therefore two forms of recognition, the one automatic, the other attentive, to which correspond two forms of memory, the one motor and "quasi instantaneous," the other representative and enduring. We should, at all costs, avoid muddling this distinction, which is made from the standpoint of the actualization of recollection, with a completely different distinction, made from the point of view of Memory in itself (recollection-memory and memory-contraction).

36. On these two types of disturbance, cf. three essential texts, MM, 99 (245, 108), 110 (253, 118), 174 (314, 196). In this last text Bergson distinguishes

between mechanical and dynamic disturbances.

37. Cf. MM, 108 (253, 119): "The evocation of recollections themselves is hindered" (translation modified); and also MM, 97-98 (245, 108).

38. MM, 175 (314, 196).

39. ME, 177-183 (925-928, 146-150).

40. ME, 130 (896, 107).

CHAPTER IV

1. Cf. above pp. 27-29.

2. MM, 79 (225, 83): "We pass, by imperceptible stages, from recollections strung out along the course of time to the movements which indicate their nascent or possible action in space...." MM, 122 (266, 135): "We have here a continuous movement.... At no moment is it possible to say with precision that the idea or the recollection-image ends, that the recollection-image or the sensation begins." Translation modified. MM, 125-126 (270, 140): "To the degree that these recollections take the form of a more complete, more concrete and more conscious representation, they tend to confound themselves with the perception which attracts them or of which they adopt the outline."

3. MM, 151 (292, 168).

4. On going beyond the two dualisms: (1) quantity-quality, (2) extended-nonextended, cf. MM, Chs. 1 and 4.

5. On the movement belonging to things as much as to the Self, cf. MM, 198 (331, 219); 204 (340, 230).

6. *Reintroduction of the theme of degrees and intensities*: Cf. MM, Ch. 4, passim, and 222 (355, 250): "Between brute matter and the mind most capable of reflection there are all possible intensities of memory or, what comes to the same thing, all the degrees of freedom." CE, 219 (665, 201): "Our feeling of duration, I should say the actual coinciding of our self with itself, admits of degrees." And already in TF, 239-240 (156, 180): "It is because the transition is made by imperceptible steps from concrete duration, whose ele-

ments permeate one another, to symbolical duration whose moments are set side by side, and consequently from free activity to conscious automatism."

7. *Reintroduction of the theme of the negative*, both as limitation and opposition: Cf. CE, 99-100 (571ff., 90ff.), matter is both limitation of movement and obstacle to movement, "it is a negation rather than a positive reality." CE, 220 (666, 202): matter as "inversion," "interversion," "interruption...." These texts are nevertheless related to those where Bergson challenges all notion of the negative.

8. Cf. MM: on modifications and perturbations, 201 (337, 226); on irreducible rhythms, 205-206 (342, 232-233); on the absolute character of differences, 193-194 (331-332, 219).

9. CM, 217-219 (1461, 207-209). The next two quotations come from the same text, which is very important to Bergson's whole philosophy.

10. Cf. CE, 184 (637, 168).

11. CE, 13 (502, 10): "What else can this mean than that the glass of water, the sugar and the process of the sugar's melting in the water are abstractions, and that the Whole within which they have been cut out by my senses and understanding progresses in the same manner as a consciousness?" On the particular characteristic of the living being, and its resemblance to the Whole, cf. CE, 18-19 (507, 15). But *Matter and Memory* had already invoked the Whole as the condition under which we attribute a movement and a duration to things: MM, 193 (329, 216); 196 (332, 220).

12. DS, 45-46 (57-58).

13. DS, 46 (58-59). Bergson goes so far as to say that impersonal Time has only one and the same "rhythm." *Matter and Memory*, on the contrary, affirms the plurality of rhythms, the *personal* character of durations (cf. MM, 207 [342, 232]: "but neither is it that homogeneous and impersonal duration, the same for every thing and everyone..."). But there is no contradiction: In DS the diversity of *fluxes* will replace that of rhythms, for reasons of terminological precision; and impersonal Time, as we will see, is definitely not a *homogeneous* impersonal duration.

14. DS, 52 (67).

15. DS, 47 (59): "We catch ourselves dividing and multiplying our consciousness...." Translation modified. This reflexive aspect of duration brings it particularly close to a *cogito*. On triplicity, cf. DS, 54 (70): There are in fact three essential forms of continuity: that of our interior life; that of voluntary movement; and that of a movement in space.

16. DS, 52 (68) and 61 (81). Translations modified.

17. MM, 206 (341, 232).

18. DS, 47 (59). Translation modified.

19. On this hypothesis of Relativity which defines the conditions of a crucial kind of experience: Cf. DS, 71 (97), 77-78 (114), 101 (164).

20. DS, 72 (99). Translation modified. It has often been said that Bergson's reasoning involves a misunderstanding of Einstein. But Bergson's reasoning itself has also often been misunderstood. Bergson *does not confine himself* to saying: A time that is different from mine is not lived, either by me or by others, but involves an image that I give myself of others (and reciprocally). For Bergson fully admits the legitimacy of such an image in expressing the various tensions and the relations between durations *that he will constantly recognize for his own part.* What he criticizes Relativity for is something completely different: The image that I make to myself of others, or that Peter makes to himself of Paul, is then an image that cannot be lived or thought as livable without contradiction (by Peter, by Paul, *or by Peter as he imagines Paul*). In Bergsonian terms, this is not an image, it is a "symbol." If we forget this point, all of Bergson's reasoning loses its meaning. Hence, Bergson's concern to recall, at the end of DS, 156 (234): "But these physicists are not imagined as real or able to be so...."

21. DS, 76-82 (112-116).

22. DS, 85-86 (120-121).

23. Bergson therefore distinguishes four types of *simultaneity* in an order of growing depth: (1) relativist simultaneity, between distant clocks, DS, 54 (71) and 82ff. (116ff.); (2) the two simultaneities in the instant, between

event and nearby clock; (3) and also between this moment and a moment of our duration, DS, 54-58 (70-75); (4) the simultaneity of fluxes, DS, 52-53 (67-68), 60-61 (81). Merleau-Ponty clearly shows how the theme of simultaneity, according to Bergson, confirms a genuine philosophy of "coexistence" (cf. *In Praise of Philosophy*, translated by John Wild and James M. Edie, Evanston: Northwestern University Press, 1963, pp. 14ff.).

24. DS, 134 (199) and 155ff. (233ff.).

25. Cf. DS, 134 (199) and 150 (225), an attack on a "space which swallows time," of a "time which in turn absorbs space."

26. Against the idea of a space that is given to us ready made, cf. CE, 224-225 (69, 206).

27. In this sense, matter and dreams have a natural affinity, both representing a state of expansion (*détente*), in us and outside us: CE, 220-221 (665-667, 202-203).

28. CE, 221-222 (666-667, 203-204) and MM, Ch. 4, *passim*.

29. On space as scheme or schema, cf. MM, 206 (341, 232); 209-211 (344-345, 235-236); CE, 221 (667, 203).

30. Cf. CE, Ch. 3.

CHAPTER V

1. Cf. above pp. 75-76.

2. This ontological "naturalism" appears clearly in MR: On naturing Nature and natured Nature cf. 49 (1024, 56). The apparently strange notion of "nature's plan" appears in MR, 48 (1022, 54). Despite some of Bergson's expressions ("Nature intended," MR, 55 [1029, 63]), this notion should not be interpreted in too finalistic a sense: There are several *plans* and each, as we shall see, corresponds to one of the degrees or levels of contraction that all coexist in duration. Therefore, they are "planes" rather than "plans," they refer to sections, to sections of the cone rather than to a project or to an aim.

3. According to Bergson, the word "Whole" has a sense, but only on condition that it does *not* designate anything actual. He constantly recalls that:

Whole is not given. This means, not that the idea of the whole is devoid of sense, but that it designates a virtuality, actual parts do not allow themselves to be totalized.

4. Cf. CE, 99 (571, 90). And MR, 282 (1225, 313): "the essence of a vital tendency is to develop fan-wise, creating, by the mere fact of its growth, divergent directions, each of which will receive a certain proportion of the impetus." On the primacy, here, of an undivided Totality, of Unity or of a Simplicity, cf. CE, 99-101 (571-572, 90-91); 130-131 (595, 119) "the original identity."

5. CE, 109 (578, 99).

6. In fact, the products of differentiation are never completely *pure* in experience. Moreover, each line "balances" that which is exclusive in it: For example, the line that ends in intelligence arouses in intelligent beings an equivalent of instinct, a "virtual instinct" represented by *story telling*: cf. MR, 100 (1068, 114).

7. Bergson's great reproach to the philosophies of nature is that they only saw differences of degree on a single line in evolution and differentiation: CE, 149 (609, 136).

8. Philosophically, one might find in a system like Leibniz's a si.nilar hesitation between the two concepts of the virtual and of the possible.

9. Cf. CM, "The Possible and the Real."

10. CE, 72-78 (549-554, 64-70).

11. CE, 80 (555, 72): How could an external physical energy, light for example, have "converted an impression left by it into a machine capable of using it"?

12. The idea of diverging lines or of ramified series was undoubtedly not unknown to classifiers from the eighteenth century. But what matters to Bergson is the fact that the divergences of directions can only be interpreted from the perspective of the actualization of the virtual. In R. Ruyer, today, we find requirements analogous to those of Bergson: the appeal to an "inventive, mnemonic and trans-spatial potential," the refusal to interpret

evolution in purely actual terms (cf. his *Eléments de psycho-biologie*, Presses Universitaires de France).

13. When Bergson (CE, 184 [637, 168]) says, "It seems as if life, as soon as it has become bound up in a species, is cut off from the rest of its own work, save at one or two points that are of vital concern to the species just arisen. Is it not plain that life goes to work here exactly like consciousness, exactly like memory?" The reader must understand that these *points* correspond to the outstanding points that became detached at each level of the cone. Each line of differentiation or actualization thus constitutes a "plane (*plan*) of nature" that takes up again in its own way a virtual section or level (cf. note 2, above).

14. On this negative vocabulary, cf. CE, Ch. 3.

15. This character of life, posing and solution of a problem, appears to Bergson to be more important than the negative determination of need.

16. CE, 188 (640, 172); MR, 116 (1082, 132) "...at each stopping-place a combination, perfect of its kind."

17. CE, 145 (606, 132).

18. On the opposition of life and form, CE, 141 (603ff., 129ff.): "Like eddies of dust raised by the wind as it passes, the living turn upon themselves, borne up by the great blast of life. They are therefore relatively stable and counterfeit immobility so well..." On the species as "stopping place" see MR, 198 (1153, 221). This is the origin of the notion of *enclosure*, which will take on such great importance in the study of human society. The point is that, from a certain point of view, Man is no less turned in on himself, closed in on himself, circular, than the other animal species: It might be said that he is "closed." Cf. MR, 29-30 (1006, 34); 245-246 (1193, 273).

19. CE, 43-46 (526-528, 37-40).

20. Cf. DS, 137 (203ff.) on the example of the "curved plane" and of the "three dimensional curve."

21. DS, 63 (84): There is "a certain hesitation or indetermination inherent in a certain part of things" that becomes merged with "creative evolution."

22. CE, 47 (529, 41).

23. CE, 62 (541ff., 55ff.) "How do we assume that accidental causes, presenting themselves in an accidental order, have several times ended in the same result, the causes being infinitely numerous and the effect infinitely complicated?" L. Cuenot has set out all kinds of examples going in the direction of the Bergsonian theory, cf., *Invention et finalité en biologie*.

24. CE, 58 (538, 51).

25. Cf. CE, 198-199 (649, 182); ME, 8 (818ff., 5ff.).

26. MR, 200 (1154, 223).

27. On the man who tricks nature, extending beyond the "plane" (*plan*) and returning to a naturing Nature, cf. MR, 48-57 (1022-1029, 55-64). On man's going beyond his own condition, MR, passim, and CM, 229 (1425-218).

28. CE, 288 (719, 264).

29. ME, 18-20 (825-826, 14-15).

30. MR, 189-190 (1145, 211). On the story-telling function and the virtual instinct, 99 (1067ff., 113ff.) and 109-110 (1076, 124). On obligation and the virtual instinct, 20 (998, 23).

31. MR, 29-30 (1006, 34).

32. MR, 83-84 (1053, 94); 198-199 (1153, 222).

33. Bergson nevertheless suggests this explanation in certain texts, for example, MR, 200-201 (1155, 224). But it only has a provisional value.

34. MR, 31 (1008, 35). The theory of the creative emotion is all the more important as it gives affectivity a status that it lacked in the preceding works. In *Time and Free Will*, affectivity tended to become intermingled with duration in general. In *Matter and Memory*, on the contrary, it had a much more precise role, but was impure and rather painful. On the creative emotion and its relations with intuition, the reader is referred to the study of M. Gouhier, in *L'histoire et sa philosophie* (Vrin, pp. 76ff.).

35. MR, 243 (1191-1192, 270) and 30-32 (1007-1008, 35-36).

36. It will be noted that art, according to Bergson, also has two sources. There is a *story-telling* art, sometimes collective, sometimes individual: MR, 184-186 (1141-1142, 206-207). And there is an *emotive* or *creative* art: MR,

241 (1190, 268). Perhaps all art presents these two aspects, but in variable proportions. Bergson does not disguise the fact that the story-telling aspect appears to him to be inferior in art; the novel would above all be story-telling, music on the contrary, emotion and creation.

37. Cf. MR, 243 (1192, 270): "...create creators."

38. MR, 55-56 (1029, 63).

39. On the three mysticisms, Greek, Oriental and Christian, cf. MR, 205-206 (1158ff., 229ff.).

40. Cf. MR, 234 (1184, 260). Let us remember that the notion of probability has the greatest importance in the Bergsonian method, and that intuition is no less a method of exteriority than of interiority.

Index

ABSENCE, 17–18.

Absolute, the, 35, 49, 76, 84.

Abstraction, 25, 44, 46, 53, 75, 96, 98, 99.

Achilles' race, 47–48, 81.

Action, 14, 19, 24, 55, 56, 68; order of, 33; possible, 53; psychological, 56.

Actual, the, 15, 85, 93, 96, 97, 98, 101–03, 104, 106. *See also* Real.

Actualization, 14, 42–43, 52, 53, 56–57, 58, 62–71, 73, 82, 94–95, 97, 98, 103–07, 109, 111, 113; of past, 56–57; psychic, 42.

Affection, 23, 53; -subjectivity, 53.

Affectivity, 25, 56.

Affinity, natural, 27, 33.

Alteration, 31, 32, 47, 92.

Analysis, transcendental, 23.

Animal, 94, 95, 101, 109, 111.

Aphasia, 30, 69.

Articulations, 27, 28, 68; natural, 18, 22, 27, 29, 31. *See also* Real, the, articulation of.

Augmentation, 31.

Automaton, 67.

BECOMING, 37, 44, 45; -conscious, 16.

Being, 17–18, 19, 20, 35, 44, 46–47, 55–56, 61, 62–63, 76–77, 84, 85; diminution of, 23; paradox of, 61; -present, 55; pure, 59.

Berkeley, George, 41.

Biology, 94, 95, 97; taxonomy, 103–04, 105.

Body, 26, 30, 41, 69, 70–71, 103, 109.

Brain, 24, 52–55, 69, 107; faculty of, and core function, 24–25; -subjectivity, 52.

CALCULUS, 27.

Coalescence, 65, 66.

Coexistence, 59–60, 74, 77, 80–81, 86, 91, 93, 100–01, 103, 111; paradox of, 61; virtual, 60, 77, 85, 93–94.

Composite, 18–19, 22–23, 26, 28, 29–30, 32, 34, 37, 38, 47, 53, 73, 85, 86, 92, 95–96, 112; badly analyzed, 17, 18, 20, 22, 28, 54, 58, 61–62, 73, 86.

Concept, 28, 44–45, 75, 97.

Cone, metaphor of, 59–60 (fig.), 64–65, 66, 67, 88, 100.

Consciousness, 30, 42, 45, 48, 51, 52, 56, 78, 81, 82, 84, 106; planes of, 65, 66; psychological, 63; self-, 52, 106, 113.

Contemporaneity, 58, 59, 71.

Continuity, 21, 37, 38, 43, 52, 57, 87.

137

Contraction, 21, 51–52, 53, 60, 61,
64–67, 70, 74, 75, 76, 79, 82,
86–89, 93, 102, 103, 107; degrees/
levels of, 60, 74, 75, 85, 93, 100, 101;
–memory, 26, 52, 60, 74; ontological and psychological, 65; –relaxation, 75; -subjectivity, 53.
Convergence, 29, 30, 73. See also
Intersection.
Creation, 97, 98, 101, 103, 105, 106,
108, 110–12.
Creative Evolution, 37, 77, 78, 100.

DATUM, IMMEDIATE, 38, 75.
Decomposition, 38, 53, 67, 68, 92, 96.
Deterioration, 22, 23, 46, 47, 75–76,
103.
Determinism, 107.
Difference, 35, 75–76, 92, 93, 97, 98,
100; in degree, 20, 21, 22–23, 25,
31–32, 34, 35, 38, 41, 43, 45, 47,
58, 73, 74, 75, 76, 91, 92–93, 94,
96, 101; of intensity, 20–21, 75, 91,
92, 94; internal, 99; in kind, 14,
18–25, 27–35, 38, 41, 42–43, 46,
47, 54, 55, 58, 61, 73, 75–76, 81,
82, 91, 92, 93, 95, 96; in number,
35, 41; qualitative, 31.
Differentiation, 29, 35, 43, 94, 95, 97,
101–03 (fig. p. 102), 104, 106, 107,
108, 110, 113.
Dilation, see Expansion, Relaxation.
Dimension, 23.
Diminution, 23, 31.
Discontinuity, 21, 37, 51.
Disorder, 17–18, 19–20, 46–47.
Distinction, 77; extrinsic, 37–38; of
quality, 35; of quantity, 84; real, 85, 86.
Disturbance, 68–70, 71, 76; dynamic,
69; mechanical, 68.
Divergence, 28–30, 43, 53, 73, 95, 97,
100, 105–06.
Division, 22, 24, 31, 32, 40, 41–42, 47,
66, 79, 80–81, 92–96, 99, 103,
104, 112; two types of, 95–96.

Doubt, 19.
Dreams, 66, 107.
Dualism, 21–22, 29, 31, 73, 75, 76,
91, 93, 94, 96; genetic, 96; reflexive,
96.
Dualities, 74, 93.
Duration, 13–14, 19, 21, 22, 26, 28,
31–35, 37–38, 40, 42, 45–46,
48–49, 51–52, 54, 60, 75–113;
–contraction, 23, 107; dispersed,
77; external, 48; in general, 45;
intense, 77; internal, 81, 83–84,
107; multiple, 48–49, 75, 76–77,
78, 83–85; ontological, 49; psychological, 34, 37, 48–49, 76, 77; pure,
95; simultaneous, 48; single, 78.
Duration and Simultaneity, 39, 78, 85.

EGOISM, 109, 110.
Einstein, Albert. 40, 79–80, 83,
84, 85.
Élan vital, 13, 14, 16, 94, 95, 101,
104, 106, 107, 112–13.
Emotion, 18, 42, 110–12.
Energy, 76, 102.
Essai sur les éléments principaux de la
répresentation, 44.
Essence, 32, 34, 94, 110.
Eternity, 23, 55, 56, 104.
Evolution, 98, 100, 106.
Evolutionism, 23, 98–99.
Excitation, 24, 52, 107, 111.
Existence, 20, 77.
Expansion, 30, 60, 66–67, 70, 74,
75, 79, 86–89, 91, 93, 95, 100,
102, 103, 107. See also Relaxation.
Expenditure, 102.
Experience, 13, 22, 25–27, 30, 34,
37, 53, 74, 81–82, 92, 99;
conditions of, 20, 23, 25, 26, 27,
28, 30, 37, 99; physical, 47–48;
possible, 23; psychological, 33,
34, 37, 38; pure, 92; real, 23, 27,
28; turn in, 27, 28, 73, 91, 92,
93, 95.

Extension, 22, 34, 35, 42, 74–75, 79, 86, 87–88, 89, 94.
Exteriority, 49, 74–75, 77–78, 93, 99, 102, 103.

FALSITY, 16, 98.
Fictions, 25, 34, 85, 98, 108.
Finalism, 104, 105.
Flux, 80–85, 91; triple, 80–81, 82.
Form, 88, 103–04; variety of, 45.
Fourth dimension, 79, 86, 104–05.
Freedom, 15, 16, 17, 19, 51, 106, 107.
Freud, Sigmund, 55–56.
Future, the, 52.

GENERALIZATION, 44–46.
God, 104, 108, 110, 112.

HAMELIN, 44.
Hegelianism, 44.
Heterogeneity, 21, 37, 43, 74, 100.
History, 16.
Höffding, 13.
Homogeneity, 20, 21, 33, 37, 74, 100.

IDEALISM, 33, 77.
Illusions, 20, 21, 23, 33–35, 58, 61, 104.
Image, 17–18, 24, 41, 57–58, 65–68, 70, 71, 81, 97–98; recall of, 63; virtual, 28, 29.
Inadequacy, 44, 46, 75.
Indivisibles, 42. See also Division.
Inextensity, 23.
Instant, 25, 51–52, 53, 74, 84, 87, 95.
Instinct, 21, 94, 95, 101, 102, 103, 108, 110.
Intelligence, 21, 88–89, 94, 95, 102, 104, 107–10, 112; order of, 33.
Intensity, 17, 18–19, 75–76, 91–92.
Intersection, 28, 29, 30, 35, 53–54. See also Convergence.
Interval, 24, 46; cerebral, 24, 25, 52–53, 107, 109, 111.
Intuition, 21, 27, 31–32, 35, 88, 102, 109–10, 111–12; as method, 13–14,
22–24, 32, 33, 38, 73, 77.
Invention, 15–16, 35, 108, 111.

KANT, IMMANUEL, 20–21, 46.
Knowledge, 13, 17, 35.

LANGUAGE, 15, 57, 62, 68; foreign, 62; ontology of, 57.
Leap, ontological, 56, 57, 61, 62, 109; paradox of, 61.
Life, 16, 19, 52, 94–95, 101, 102, 103–04, 106, 107; attention to, 68, 70, 72, 80.

MACHINE, 107.
Man, 106, 109, 113.
Marx, Karl, 16.
Mathematics, 15–16, 27, 41–42. See also Riemann.
Matter, 21, 22, 24–27, 30, 34, 35, 41, 43, 53, 54–55, 60–61, 73, 74, 75, 77, 78, 82, 86, 87–89, 92, 93, 94, 101–03, 107–08; contraction of, 25–26; –expansion, 23; order of, 88.
Matter and Memory, 23–24, 29, 40, 41, 52–53, 72, 73, 75, 76, 78, 86, 92, 96, 100.
Meaning, 88.
Mechanism, 19, 23, 67–68, 69, 70, 98, 104, 105, 107.
Memory, 13, 21, 22, 25–26, 30, 37, 43, 51–52, 53, 55, 57, 63–64, 65, 67, 70, 73, 77, 92, 93, 100, 102, 106–07, 109, 111, 112–13; Bergson's theory of, 43, 55–56; ontological, 57, 59; paradox of, 58–59; psychophysiological theories of, 58, 61; pure, 27, 58, 74, 95; two aspects of, 51–52, 53–54.
mens momentanea, 75.
Metaphysics, 15, 20, 23, 29, 35.
Method, 13ff., 32, 38, 75, 91–92, 93, 96, 112; dialectical, 44-45. See also Intuition.
Mind, 26, 37, 62, 88, 109.

Mind-Energy, 30.
Modification, 76.
Monism, 29, 73, 74, 75, 76, 78, 82, 91, 93, 94.
Motive, psychological, 17–18.
Movement, 24, 27, 31, 43, 47, 48–49, 52, 54, 65, 67–69, 70, 71, 74, 75, 79, 82, 84, 94–95, 103–05, 106, 107; executed, 24, 52; false, 44; mechanical, 70–71; –perception, 67–69; received, 24, 52, 74, 87, 92.
Multiple, the, 39, 43–44, 45–46, 47, 76, 80, 85, 93; unity of, 44, 45, 93–94.
Multiplicity, 14, 32, 38ff., 47, 49, 78, 79–80, 85; abstract, 45; actual/ spatial, 85; continuous/qualitative, 38, 39–40, 42–43, 47, 80, 81; discontinuous/quantitative, 38, 40, 41, 43, 47, 80; discrete, 39; two kinds of, 19, 21, 38ff., 47, 53, 79–80, 85; virtual/temporal, 82–83, 85, 112–13.
Mysticism, 112.

Nature, 19, 34, 80, 93, 107, 108–09, 110, 113.
nature naturanta, 93.
nature naturée, 93.
Need, 62, 68, 108; order of, 33; -subjectivity, 52.
Negation, 18, 19, 46, 52, 75–76; generalized, 17, 46.
Negative, the, 18, 46, 75–76, 101–03; of limitation and of opposition, 46–47.
Nonbeing, 17–18, 19–20, 44, 46–47.
Nothingness, 20, 23.
Novelty, 20, 61.
Number, potential, 40–41, 42–43, 45.

Object, 24–25, 33, 40–41, 47, 52, 53, 68, 73, 75, 77, 78, 110; image of, 41.
Objectivity, 30, 33, 40–41, 43, 53, 54.

Obligation, 108.
Observation, 30.
One, the, 39, 43–44, 45–46, 47, 80, 85, 93, 100.
Ontology, 34–35, 49, 56, 76.
Opposition, 44–45, 46, 75–76, 82, 96, 101.
Order, 17–18, 46–47.
Organism, 16, 105.

Paramnesia, 71.
Participation, 77–78, 88.
Past, the, 25, 37, 54ff., 70, 71, 73, 74, 75, 91, 92; in general, 56–57, 59, 61, 62–64; image of, 51; degrees/ levels of, 59–67, 74, 77; preservation of, 25, 51, 54–55, 59; pure, 59, 74, 75, 95, 109; regions of, 56–57, 58, 61–66; totality of, 27, 61, 62.
Pedagogy, 15.
Perception, 21, 23–25, 26–27, 30, 51, 53, 58, 63, 67–68, 73, 74, 75, 107; actual, 41, 67; -image, 58, 66, 67–68, 71, 73, 74, 95; –object– matter, 26; Pure, 26, 27, 28, 54, 55, 58; Real, 25; –recollection, 22, 29; virtual, 25, 41.
Perfection, 23, 103.
Philosophy, 13, 14, 27–28, 44–45, 46, 75, 94, 99, 111–13.
Physics, 35. *See also* Einstein.
Plant, 94, 95, 101, 102, 110.
Plato, 32, 44–45, 59.
Pluralism, 76, 77–78, 83–84, 104; generalized, 77–78, 82; limited, 77–78, 82; quantitative, 76.
Plurality, 14, 24.
Point, 79; mathematical, 25, 53; of unity, 73–74, 93; virtual, 28, 29, 30, 112.
Position, 23.
Possibility, 18, 19, 43, 96.
Possible, the, 17–18, 20, 24, 41, 47, 96–98; Leibnizian, 71.

Precision, 13, 14, 29, 40, 94.
Preformism, 98.
Presence, 22–23, 26.
Present, the, 25, 48, 51–52, 54ff., 68, 70–75, 88, 91, 92; pure, 74, 95.
Probabilism, 30.
Problems, 15ff., 21, 29; badly stated, 17, 18–19, 21; creation/statement of, 14, 15–17, 21, 31, 35; false, 15–17, 18, 20, 23–24, 26, 33–35, 43, 54, 75, 98, 104; nonexistent, 17, 19–20; true, 15–17, 33.
Proportion, 23, 31.
Proust, Marcel, 85, 96.
Psychology, 26, 57, 76.
Pure, the, 22, 49, 52.

QUALITY, 21, 31, 32, 48, 51, 53, 74, 87–88, 92; heterogeneous, 74.
Quantity, 21, 74, 91; homogeneous, 74.
Questions, badly stated, 17, 24.

REAL, THE, 17, 21, 29, 30, 41, 44, 47, 96–98, 108; articulation of, 26, 92; disarticulation of, 30.
Realism, 33, 77.
Reality, 22, 34, 42, 45, 97, 100; nonpsychological, 56; psychological, 34, 58.
Realization, 20, 41, 43, 71, 96–97.
Reason, 20, 108; sufficient, 28–29, 86.
Recognition, 67, 68, 69.
Recollection, 21–27, 30, 37, 51, 53, 54, 56–57, 58, 61–73, 107; -image, 58, 63, 65–68, 70, 71, 73, 74, 95, 109; –memory, 26, 52, 60, 74; –perception, 22; pure, 26, 55, 56, 62, 63, 66, 68, 69, 70, 71, 74; -subjectivity, 53; virtual, 56, 63, 71.
Recomposition, 45, 57.
Relativity, theory of, 39, 79, 83–84, 86.
Relaxation, 21, 23, 60, 61, 65, 74, 75, 76, 79, 82, 87–89, 95; levels, degrees of, 60, 74, 75, 85, 86, 88–89, 91, 100. See also Expansion.
Religion, 34, 108.
Reminiscence, 62; 111; Plato's theory of, 59.
Repetition, 51, 60–61, 68, 93; physical and psychic, 60–61, paradox of, 61; virtual, 61.
Representation, 22, 24, 53, 66, 87, 108, 110.
Repression, 21, 72.
Resemblance, 101, 105–06.
Response, 24, 107, 111.
Rest, 79.
Riemann, G.B.R., 39–40, 79.
Rotation, 64, 65–66, 68, 69, 70; –orientation, 64.
Rules, 15, 17, 21, 29, 31.

SCHEME, DYNAMIC, 66, 69; motor, 67–68, 69, 70.
Science, 14, 20, 23, 35, 40, 86.
Section, discontinuous, 37; instantaneous, 54.
Self, 44, 75, 106.
Sensations, 18–19, 53, 74, 75, 87.
Sense, 88.
Simultaneity, 48, 79, 80–81, 84–85; of fluxes, 81, 89.
Simplicity, 43, 46, 94, 95, 96, 100.
Sleep, 66–67.
Society, 15, 108–11.
Solution, 15–17, 21, 29–30, 103; false, 20.
Soul, 112; immortality of, 30.
Sources, two kinds of, 21.
Space, 19, 21, 22, 25, 31–38, 43, 47, 49, 60, 75, 79, 86–88, 92, 104–05; auxiliary, 38; homogeneous, 34; order of, 34; pure, 88, 89; real, 105; scientific conception of, 40; –time, 79, 85, 95, 104–05.
Spirit, 30, 35, 93.
Story-telling function, 108–111.

Subject, 42, 48, 73, 81–82, 83.
Subjectivity, 26, 30, 33, 40, 42–43,
   53; five aspects of, 52–53.
Succession, 25, 45, 48, 59, 60, 81;
   internal, 37.
Sugar, lump of, 31–32, 77.
Systems, closed, 18, 43, 77; fixed and
   mobile, 79.

TENDENCY, 21, 22–23, 28, 31, 32,
   92, 93, 99; motor, 67, 68.
Tension, 60, 74, 76, 79, 86, 87, 88,
   95; levels of, 77.
Time, 22, 31, 32, 43, 58–59, 61–62,
   74, 75, 78, 79ff., 85–86, 93,
   104–05; multiplicity of, 76, 78,
   79, 83–84, 85; relativistic, 79–80,
   83–84; real, 14, 78, 79; single, 80,
   81, 82–83, 85, 91, 93, 100;
   spatialized, 22, 23, 80, 85, 86, 104.
   See also Instant.
Time and Free Will, 37, 39, 40, 43, 48,
   53, 60, 76, 78, 79, 91, 96.

Totality, 32, 105; virtual, 93, 95, 100.
Translation, 63–64, 65–66, 68, 69, 70,
   97; –contraction, 64, 70.
Truth, 16, 18, 29, 34.

UNCONSCIOUS, 42, 55–56, 71–72;
   Freudian, 55–56; ontological, 71;
   psychological, 55–56, 71; virtual, 55.
Unity, ontological, 74, 93, 95, 100.
Universe, 78; Whole of, 77, 78, 82,
   100, 103, 104, 105, 112.
Utility, 27, 55, 64, 67, 68, 70–71, 88,
   99, 106, 107, 109.

VIBRATION, *see* Movement, received.
Virtual, the, 15, 42–43, 56, 57, 60,
   63, 81, 82, 85, 94, 95, 96, 97–98,
   100, 103, 104, 105, 106; pure, 62.
Virtuality, 41, 82–83, 93, 95, 97,
   99–100, 101, 103, 106, 113.

WILL, 19.

This edition designed by Bruce Mau
Type composed by Archie at Canadian Composition